WHAT YOUR COLLEAGUES ARE SAYING . . .

"*Teaching Writing From Content to Career* offers useful tools and techniques that you can put to work immediately, while inviting you throughout the book to pause and reflect on what you and your students are trying out in your classroom. The authors routinely connect their concepts and content to the world beyond school for which we are always preparing our students."

—Jim Burke, Author
Teaching Better Day by Day and
The Six Academic Writing Assignments: Designing the User's Journey

"Don't go to school without this book! It is chock-full of ideas, tools, and engaging lessons for teaching writing to middle and high school students. It is just the resource you need to ensure your students write well in and out of the classroom."

—Steve Graham, Regents and Warner Professor
Arizona State University

"Grant, Lapp, and Thayre have developed a book that allows teachers to reflect upon writing beyond the ELA classroom – then teach the necessary skills. These authors bridge practicality with theory and research, something that is much needed in professional literature. Their insight and ideas into fostering confident and competent writers is inspiring and timely."

—Rebecca G. Harper, Associate Professor of Literacy
Augusta University, and
Author, *Writing Workouts* and *Write Now & Write On*

"Grant, Lapp, and Thayre's book bravely tackles a necessary (yet often humbling) question: Why do our students really need to write? Both now, and in a future that is getting harder for us all to predict? The authors patiently show us how teachers can ensure that our approach to writing instruction remains focused on these real-world applications. *Teaching Writing From Content Classroom to Career* offers no shortage of concrete lesson examples; my favorite is the one about how students (and teachers!) might best write an email that is not only clear and understandable, but also strikes a friendly enough tone—something that students in my classes always need instruction on. The authors also provide a refreshingly honest take on the role of artificial intelligence models in writing instruction, going so far as to include Chat GPT prompts in a lesson plan and how to refine the prompting process. Overall, this is an important, timely book—one that will remain useful for a long time."

—Matthew R. Kay, ELA Teacher and Author
Not Light but Fire: How to Lead Meaningful Race Conversations in the Classroom,
and Co-Author, *Answers to Your Biggest Questions About Teaching Middle- and High School ELA*

"The overall focus of this book and the importance of considering purpose and audience is fresh and inspiring. I haven't seen other professional literature on the subject, and it's becoming more vital every day. We must prepare students for THEIR future and stop parroting what and how we were taught."

—Ruthanne Munger, Writing Specialist
Union School Corporation
Modoc, IN

"This book provides clear explanations on the meaning of writing purpose, of audience, and of the writing process with scenarios and examples that allow teachers to see the transformation of guidelines to actionable items. Through embedded stopping points, the teacher is asked to take the position of the writer -- and write as their students will. The text and its stopping points are well designed, making the book interactive, clear on its meanings, and equipping teachers with skills and knowledge to help students write well beyond classroom contexts."

—Zoi Philippakos, Associate Professor
Literacy Education
University of Tennessee, Knoxville

"In *Teaching Writing From Content to Career*, Grant, Lapp, and Thayre have skillfully crafted a book that shifts writing instruction from a "one day you'll need this" to "see how you'll need this" approach. This is so needed in classrooms that are determined to meet true, useful writing expectations postsecondary writing students will encounter."

—Andy Schoenborn, National Writing Project Teacher Consultant
Co-Author, *Creating Confident Writers: For High School, College, and Life*

"This is a book every teacher should read. We sometimes forget that there is a world out there beyond our standards because we do have so much to cover. If we can shift, as the authors suggest, to a curriculum built around student interest and their ideas for their future careers, we can better evaluate their mastery in a way that is effective for our classes as well as relevant to their lives. Students will be more engaged and will develop a sense of agency well before many of us did."

—Melissa Wood-Glusac, ELA Teacher
Thousand Oaks High School, Thousand Oaks, CA and
Co-Director, CSUN Writing Project

Teaching Writing From Content Classroom to Career, Grades 6–12

Teaching Writing From Content Classroom to Career, Grades 6–12

Maria C. Grant

Diane Lapp

Marisol Thayre

CORWIN Literacy

FOR INFORMATION:

Corwin
A SAGE Company
2455 Teller Road
Thousand Oaks, California 91320
(800) 233-9936
www.corwin.com

SAGE Publications Ltd.
1 Oliver's Yard
55 City Road
London EC1Y 1SP
United Kingdom

SAGE Publications India Pvt. Ltd.
Unit No 323–333, Third Floor, F-Block
International Trade Tower Nehru Place
New Delhi 110 019
India

SAGE Publications Asia-Pacific Pte. Ltd.
18 Cross Street #10-10/11/12
China Square Central
Singapore 048423

Vice President and
 Editorial Director: Monica Eckman
Executive Editor: Tori Mello Bachman
Content Development Editor: Sharon Wu
Editorial Assistant: Zack Vann
Project Editor: Amy Schroller
Copy Editor: Lynne Curry
Typesetter: C&M Digitals (P) Ltd.
Proofreader: Jeff Bryant
Indexer: Integra
Cover Designer: Janet Kiesel
Marketing Manager: Margaret O'Connor

This book is printed on acid-free paper.

23 24 25 26 27 10 9 8 7 6 5 4 3 2 1

Contents

Visit the companion website at
resources.corwin.com/ClassroomToCareer
for downloadable resources.

Acknowledgments

The authors wish to acknowledge wonderful Corwin editors and managers like Amy Schroller and Margaret O'Connor who make writing a book such an enjoyable task.

A very special thank you is reserved for Tori Mello Bachman who believed in the idea of this book and offered endless counsel and positive tips throughout its development.

Hats off to each of you!

With so much appreciation, Maria, Diane, Marisol

Publisher Acknowledgments

Corwin gratefully acknowledges the contributions of the following reviewers:

Andy Schoenborn
English Teacher
Clare Public Schools
Midland, MI

Melissa Wood Glusac
English Teacher
Thousand Oaks High School
Thousand Oaks, CA

Ruthanne Munger
Writing Specialist—Grades K–12
Union School Corporation
Modoc, IN

About the Authors

Maria C. Grant, EdD, is a professor in the Department of Secondary Education at California State University Fullerton and the director of the Single Subject Credential Program at CSUF. She works with both pre-service and in-service teachers in the credential program and at school sites. Her work includes research and publications in the areas of disciplinary literacy, literacy in the content areas, science education, and pedagogy. In addition to her efforts at the university, Maria's experience includes many years of teaching in high school and middle school science classrooms. She has taught physics, oceanography, coordinated science, chemistry, and earth science. She currently supports learners as teacher and coach at Health Sciences High & Middle College. Over the years, Maria has acted as a leader in curriculum development and professional development at both the school and district levels. Her most recent efforts include research and professional development work centered on reading, writing, and language within content classrooms. Maria can be reached at mgrant@fullerton.edu. Follow her on X at @mgrantfullerton

Diane Lapp, EdD, is a distinguished professor of education at San Diego State University where her work continues to be applied to schools. She is also an instructional coach and teacher at Health Sciences High & Middle College. Throughout her career, Diane has taught in elementary, middle, and high schools. Her major areas of research and instruction regard issues related to the planning and assessment of very intentional literacy instruction and learning.

A member of both the California and the International Reading Halls of Fame, Diane has authored, coauthored, and edited numerous articles, columns, texts, handbooks, and children's materials on instruction, assessment, and literacy related issues. Diane can be reached at lapp@sdsu.edu. Follow her on X @lappsdsu

Marisol Thayre, PhD, is a secondary English teacher, author, and instructional coach. She has worked with preservice and experienced teachers alike in creating purposeful, collaborative, and data-driven classrooms for various grade levels and content areas. In addition to her role as a teacher leader and mentor, Marisol has presented both nationally and internationally on topics including assessment, secondary literacy strategies, differentiation, and collaboration. Her current research endeavors are focused on the integration of social emotional learning into content-area instruction. Marisol currently teaches high school English and college composition in San Diego, California.

What Happens in English Language Arts Class Shouldn't Stay There

. . . The English language is a multifaceted oration

Subject to indefinite transformation

—Jamila Lyiscott, "3 Ways to Speak English"

To write well, express yourself like the common people, but think like a wise man.

—Aristotle

A writer, I think, is someone who pays attention to the world.

—Susan Sontag

Writing is often a source of anxiety and confusion for both students and adults alike. It can be difficult to know where to start when asked to compose a piece of text, let alone manage the courage to eventually share it with someone else. This is problematic for a variety of reasons, since we know that, beyond the college requirements for writing, writing is a common tool used in almost every workplace setting. Therefore, it becomes an urgent task to find ways to develop our students' confidence in their own writing process, so that they will be empowered in their chosen careers. People who approach the writing process with apprehension are more likely to deliver a subpar end product (J. Daly, 1978; J. Daly & Miller, 1975; Faigley, et al., 1981; McCarthy et al., 1985), and writing anxiety can even go on to influence the types of majors students choose (Wiltse, 2006). The aim of this book is to explore ways in which you, the teacher, can guide your students through a purpose-based writing process that will equip them with the skills and confidence to address writing tasks in and out of the classroom. We believe students should leave school with the realization that no matter what plans they have for their futures, they will be asked every day to communicate their ideas when talking, reading, and writing.

The prerequisite for writing effectively is to know what you want to say, why you want to say it, and who you want to hear it. Writing without personal meaning and writing without an authentically chosen audience turns purposeful writing into a nebulous writing task. Additionally, it's essential to understand and acknowledge that language is regional, situational, and community based. Not all scenarios that demand writing can be addressed with a formulaic approach. Instead, apprentice writers need to learn to assess audience and purpose before they even begin to outline their approach to a piece of writing. What's more, our understanding of "conventional" writing norms is evolving as we learn to embrace the diverse ways in which different communities approach language. While traditional academic writing may be appropriate in some workplace settings, in others it may be considered cold, detached, or simply not effective for the audience and task at hand. Instead of teaching students that there is one "right" way to approach an audience, what if we taught them how to assess what their connection to the purpose and audience is, and then select the best approach to reach them? As part of this introduction we quote Trinidadian American poet Jamila Lyiscott whose spoken word poem reminds us that language is dynamic and ever changing, which means our approaches to writing should be too.

Lyiscott points out the real-world application aspect of language: part of being a successful communicator is knowing how and when to move in and out of different modes of speech. She addresses the need to flexibly use all of one's language resources to be understood and valued in different arenas. To understand this a bit better let's consider both the practices of code-switching and translanguaging. Code-switching, which was explained well by Joos (1962) in his book, *Five Clocks*, typically refers to the practice of switching between two or more languages or language varieties within a single conversation.

Translanguaging on the other hand refers to a broader use of language and language varieties to support communication, learning, and meaning making. Translanguaging involves the practice of flexibly using multiple languages and semiotic and linguistic resources to achieve one's goals during a communication. For example, a multilingual speaker may use translanguaging in their writing by combining their knowledge of multiple languages and semiotics, signs and symbols, such as diagrams and symbols, to more effectively convey their ideas. This speaker is using their multilingualism and their knowledge of multiple modes to convey their ideas.

Researchers García and Lin (2017) explain the following:

> Translanguaging should also be seen differently from code-switching. Code-switching, even to those scholars who see it as linguistic mastery (see, for example, Auer, 2005; Gumperz, 1982; Myers-Scotton, 2005), it is based on the monoglossic view that bilinguals have two separate linguistic systems. Translanguaging, however, posits the linguistic behavior of bilinguals as being always heteroglossic (see Bakhtin, 1981; S. Bailey, 2015; Bailey, 2007), always dynamic, responding not to two monolingualisms in one, but to one integrated linguistic system. It is precisely because translanguaging takes up this heteroglossic and dynamic perspective centered on the linguistic use of bilingual speakers themselves, rather than starting from the perspective of named languages (usually national or state languages), that it is a much more useful theory for bilingual education than code-switching.

According to researcher-scholar Rodriguez-Valls (2023), translanguaging involves empowering students to use their linguistic repertoires without the constraints of using one named language at a time. Rodriguez-Valls shares these examples: *I like esta paleta* and *This tree is grander than the other.* Translanguaging promotes the fluidity of language. As we grow to embrace the assets that all our students bring to the classroom in terms of language, we must consider the promotion of language fluidity to create and promote a message or a written idea. To contrast, code-switching involves changing from one language to another depending on the audience, the purpose, or the context. Rodriguez-Valls offers this example: A student speaks in Spanish to other students in her project group but switches to English when presenting to the teacher and the whole class. Translanguaging skills are not skills to be taught; rather they are linguistic assets that students bring to the classroom (Dover & Rodriguez-Valls, 2022). While we should teach students to pay attention to purpose, audience, language, structure and evidence, and revision and editing, we should also embrace the linguistic riches they bring to the classroom. These two concepts, while related, differ in that translanguaging refers to a broader and more strategic and integrated use of multiple languages and language variations to support one's communication goals.

In a math classroom where the teacher and the students are speakers of both English and Spanish, the teacher may use translanguaging strategies by drawing on the students' cultural and linguistic backgrounds and multiple forms of representation. First, the teacher might introduce the math concept in English with the support of visual aids such as diagrams and graphs. Next, she might model the concept by sharing some of the key concepts in Spanish or whatever additional languages they all speak. Finally, she could ask the students to communicate as pairs or in small groups to solve the problem in both English and Spanish and to include any semiotic representations they feel support their thinking. In this way she is encouraging them to use all of their language resources to solve and share the problem.

As educators, we support both code-switching and translanguaging since we believe one can never have too much language or knowledge about language use. Instead of privileging one method of communication, we want to encourage you to ask students to capitalize on their various funds of knowledge, including their language knowledge, to meet their audience and purpose.

PAUSE AND CONSIDER

What language practices do your students already bring to the classroom? To answer this, consider their interactions. Whom do they talk with? What are they talking about? What are the styles they use for these communications? How can these be leveraged in the teaching of writing? Jot down any ideas regarding how you might encourage your students to use and broaden their language practices. Revisit these ideas as you read through the chapter.

____

____

____

____

____

____

Many take for granted that one must know how to read and speak well to communicate effectively. But we posit that to be a success in most jobs one needs to know how to write well, too. In fact, in a study compiled by the National Association of Colleges and Employers, **73.4 percent of employers** said they wanted employees with strong written communication skills because, *Clear writing is a sign of clear thinking. Great writers know how to communicate. They make things easy to understand. They can put themselves in someone else's shoes. They know what to omit. And those are qualities you want in any candidate. Writing is making a comeback all over our society . . . (Fried & Hansson, 2010).*

Think about it! Are we preparing our students to be these workers? As students, we completed many teacher-assigned writing tasks intended to teach us to think and to share our thinking, often as arguments, debates, essays, stories, and poems. We were usually taught the nuances of each genre in the process of completing the assignment. To support us, our teachers shared model texts and posted sentence frames to illustrate examples of the desired language and format. Many of us learned to write these styles fairly well. Those of us who attended college were tasked with similar assignments, and, hopefully, we got even better at writing these genres. Then, off we went into the world of work, where we are sometimes asked to write within these same genres—probably not so many stories unless we chose film writing as a career, and we are seldom asked to write poems unless we are sending a greeting card to a friend or crafting a roast for a colleague.

You might wonder then, instead of the five-paragraph essay, what are folks writing at work, and how did the preparatory writing courses and assignments they did in school prepare them to succeed? Wolsey and Lapp (2017) asked many professionals what they write at work. One re-emerging theme from this study was that while the features and practices of writing required when working in various disciplines vary, all of the professionals who were interviewed noted how important it was for them to be able to communicate complex ideas specific to their fields with nonexperts, as well as other experts in their profession or discipline.

Realizing this need for good workplace writers, we wondered what type of writing instruction should occur across disciplines in order to prepare students for the unknown writing tasks that lay ahead of them. To be able to share some specific instructional practices, we continued asking additional professionals what type of writing they were required to do at work. We wanted to extend the insights provided from related work (Gallagher, 2011; Graham & Perin, 2007; Shanahan & Shanahan, 2008; Wolsey et al., 2019) with a view toward instruction that prepares students to flexibly use the knowledge they learn in school to craft their future workplace and situational texts. To share what we learned—and help you put it into practice in your classroom—we've organized this text into six chapters and an appendix with sample lesson plans shared by the people we interviewed. Each chapter highlights an area to consider when writing any type of text. For example, we address the purpose for writing, the audience of focus, the language structure and format, evidence to support the writing intent, and the continuous evaluation via feedback. While each of these areas is highlighted in its separate chapter, we do not believe they are addressed separately when writing since writing involves a recursive process with the writer moving fluidly among these areas.

PAUSE AND CONSIDER

Before you begin reading each of these chapters, which we hope will support your instruction, we invite you to consider the following question: What kind of writing do you believe people do beyond high school? Notice if your responses grow broader as you read the scenarios we've shared throughout the book.

____

____

____

____

____

____

____

Our goal is to augment the great teaching you are already doing by sharing sample lessons, tools, and ideas you can use to illustrate to students that any written presentation must change according to its purpose and audience. We offer some instructional ideas to support you teaching students about selecting the appropriate register, tone, voice, audience, organization, and style that can prepare for their future worlds of work. You'll be able to guide students through understanding, then producing the types of associated writing they may be asked to craft in the workplace. Through broadening their exposure and deepening their insights as you question, model, and share examples it will become obvious to students that writing *does* happen after high school—and even though the finished assignment may look different than the traditional five paragraph essay, they can confidently apply what they have learned in English class to any new writing situation.

EXPANDING HOW WE TEACH (AND LEARN) WRITING

Remember when you first learned to lace your shoes? It was a painstaking, thoughtful endeavor in which you followed a pattern that was shown to you many times, over and over again. Finally, you mastered lacing, and henceforth, it became an effortless endeavor. You became highly fluent (Hattie, 2008). Perhaps you are one of the many who seek to lace your shoes in fancy or varied ways—the straight bar, the biker-hiker lace, the sawtooth, checkerboard lacing, or the complex woven lacing for special occasions. To learn a new way to lace shoes, you again have to go through the process of thinking through the patterns. You eventually learn, though, that there is a functional reason for each type of lace. Some are better for skateboarding or riding a bike; some just look interesting. Once you know the intent and the possibilities, you can choose the pattern that is most suitable, and you might be in a better position to invent your own lacing technique.

Although writing isn't the same as lacing shoes, the effort that goes into learning how to write in various ways and learning about the myriad ways writing can be used can help build learning at a deeper level and add the same kind of value through gained expertise. Hattie (2008) explains, "When a student attains a high degree of fluency on a topic, then they have more cognitive resources to devote to the next phase in learning" (p. 30). Deliberate practice makes a difference. van Gog et al. (2005) point out that "Deliberate practice requires students to stretch themselves to a higher level of performance" (p. 75). Hattie references Charness et al. (2005), who notes that "all this practice leads to higher levels of conscious monitoring and control, that leads to more refinement, and more higher order understandings of the surface and deeper level notions." Simply put, more exposure to writing practice for a variety of purposes will help our students sharpen their writing skills, which will translate to higher self-efficacy and better writing overall.

Practice in a variety of world situations will lead to deeper levels of understanding about the process of writing in various situations. Deliberate practice leads to surface and deep-level understandings and thus makes transfer learning possible. Once you have mastered checkerboard lacing to compliment the black-and-white pattern of your sneakers, you know how to learn and how to transfer your learning appropriately to any situation. Using the notions of process, practice, and transfer, classroom teachers can support students to take on writing in whatever circumstance they find themselves in.

We asked you to envision what people write at work and in their post–high school lives and how preparatory writing courses and assignments prepare them to succeed? A continuing theme from our studies (Wolsey & Lapp, 2017; Wolsey et al., 2019) was that while writing practices vary in work settings, it was noted by all of the professionals who were interviewed that being able to express complex ideas in writing is a must. Our school-learned skills are valuable, but our curriculum may need a bit of expanding to support students in thinking about what is the *just right* writing for the specific task. Students need experience in transferring skills learned in the classroom to their future world spaces, whether as citizens expressing their political or social views to a congressperson or as workers composing an informative email to a new client on behalf of their firm.

With this realization, we wondered what type of writing instruction should occur across disciplines in middle and high school to prepare students for the unknown writing tasks that lay ahead. When students tell us that they don't like to read or write, our job as educators is to help them understand the reasons why being proficient in these literacies helps them in school and beyond. To promote this understanding, our students need to know how to write real-world texts well by critiquing them and practicing how to craft them.

Let's teach students that their writing is dynamic and evolving and that there are various dialects, genres, styles, and vocabularies used when writing. Let's show them that writing resides in unique ways within cultures, generations, and in industries. **There is not just one correct way to write.** Let's model respect and hold regard for the many ways that people communicate in our world. To accomplish these goals, this book, therefore, is not about teaching students to write the *right way* or the *academic way*. It is, instead, about guiding students to notice language, tone, and style. It is about identifying purpose and audience. It is about finding the best way to communicate to particular groups of people for a purposeful reason.

The premise that foregrounds the instructional ideas shared in this text is that writing is likely to be a critical part of getting, keeping, and being promoted in most jobs (Human Factor, 2023). More importantly, it is a foundational part of sharing ideas and informing others. Or, as noted by Graham and Perin, "Writing well is not just an option for young people—it is a necessity. Along with reading comprehension, writing skill is a predictor of academic success and a basic requirement for participation in civic life and in the global economy" (2007, p. 3). As their teachers, we must identify real-world writing purposes and then revamp our current instruction to illustrate that writing is a valued skill to learn and use throughout life.

THE PATHWAY TO PURPOSEFUL WRITING FROM CLASSROOM TO CAREER

Educators must and can go beyond formulaic writing models to support future writers in thinking about relevant, meaningful ways to convey ideas and express thoughts. The base can be laid in these familiar genres, but what has been taught about audience, tone, style, and structure must be transferred and expanded to new situations if workplace writing is to be met with success.

We believe this transfer can be accomplished by considering situational writing tasks that prepare students for the writing tasks they may encounter after high school. Most students are not seeking careers as professional writers, so the significant goal of writing instruction should be to get students to share the ideas they have in an identified written form using the style, tone, and language that is appropriate for the situation.

To accomplish this, what's shared in the chapters of this book can provide a schema for teaching these crucial elements that will inform a person's writing. If we can help young people think about the purpose and use of words to send a message in a way that is best received by an intended audience, they are empowered to let their ideas be heard.

Effective writing has a dynamic nature. The audience, circumstance, tone, and mode of dissemination will change, but the intent will remain the same—to communicate. Today we communicate through message apps, email, blog posts, shared documents, and by other means. The future may offer us an even wider array of modes of written communication. Because of this dynamic nature, knowing one style of writing won't be sufficient to support the writing tasks a person needs to do. As educators, we must consider how we can help students figure out how to write for a particular purpose and how to produce a resulting piece of writing that achieves this purpose.

We propose that students need to be taught to think critically about the areas shown within each segment of the schema in Figure 0.1. Addressing these areas fluidly and interactively will support students' writing for various purposes. This schema will guide the focus of each chapter. While one area will be given the major focus in each chapter, all of the areas are at play in every chapter because writing is a recursive process that involves the continuous interaction among these areas (A. N. Applebee, 1984).

The schema which highlights a focus area within a chapter is therefore intended to guide students to address key questions about that area during the writing process. Each question shown in a block of the schema correlates with a chapter of this book:

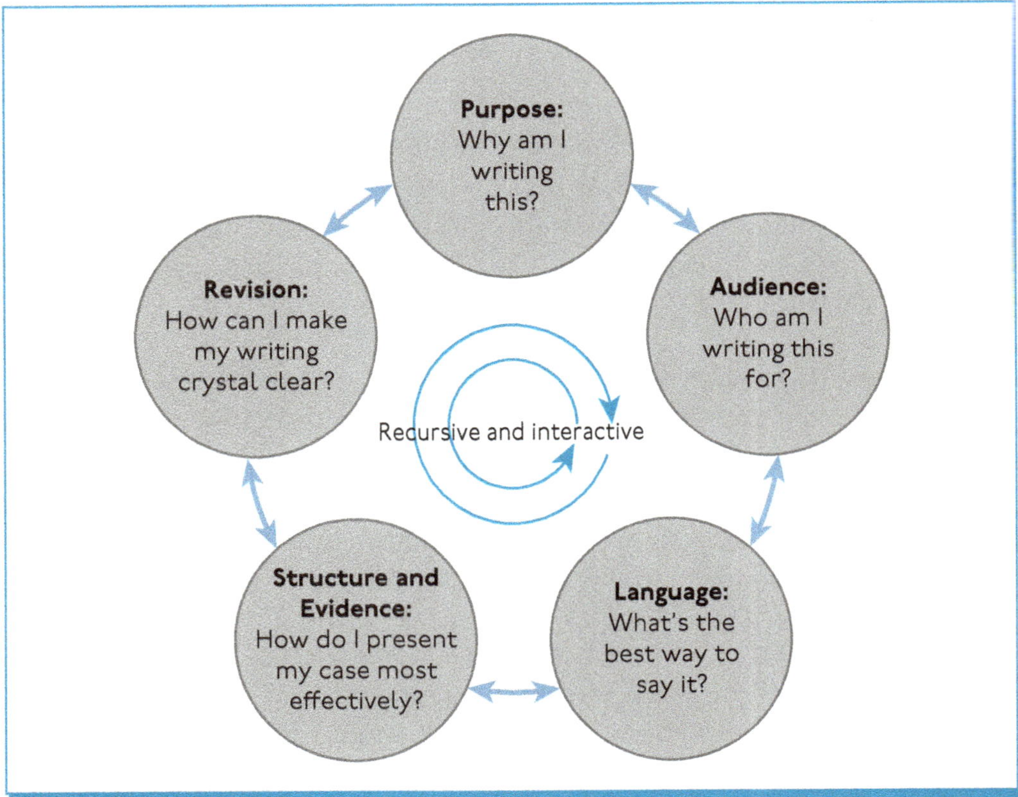

- The first question addresses the purpose by asking, *Why am I writing this?* To address this question, students are guided to think about why they are writing, how they can use model texts to support their writing, while also identifying what tools like graphic organizers they could use to support their writing.

- When considering the audience, students ask *Who am I writing for?* as they consider how to analyze and use model texts to address an audience.

- When asking *What's the best way to say it?* students think about language registers, language varieties, and writing practice.

- *How do I present my case most effectively?* is a question that guides students to consider the structure of the text being composed and to review evidence to support their writing. As they determine appropriate structures for a target audience, they will learn to pay attention to text features.

- Finally, students will be guided to ask *How can I make my writing crystal clear? How can I use feedback to revise my work?* A final look-through is essential before finalizing and sharing. Students need to understand feedback and how to use it to polish their final product.

HOW TO USE THIS BOOK

In this book, you'll discover ways that students can learn from their environments and particular situations. We will consider various means to teach writing for careers and college and offer suggestions and strategies. You'll find ideas for supporting relevant writing beyond the classroom for middle and high school students. Each chapter focuses on one aspect to consider when writing. We share tips for instruction, including teaching strategies, rubrics for student self-assessment and teacher assessment. You'll be able to use these ideas to teach any aspect of the schema you are planning to focus on in your classroom. Our goal is not to teach one way of writing but instead to promote the growth and development of critical thinkers who can flexibly navigate a changing world of writing communication.

Finally, every chapter provides instructional moves to guide and support students to become observant, critical learners and readers who can identify the purpose of a writing task, the audience, the tone, the language, the format, and the style needed to best communicate in their professional lives. Also included in each chapter are self-assessment rubrics that students can use to evaluate their communication knowledge and performance. With this information, they can identify alone or with their teachers their growing knowledge of language use and how to monitor and support themselves in current and future situations where their success depends on their abilities to communicate well.

Additionally, we have included a *points to consider* chart to support your lesson planning (Figure 0.2; also downloadable from the companion website, resources.corwin.com/ClassroomToCareer). The chart begins by inviting you to consider your lesson focus as you identify the standards your lesson will address, your learning intentions, and success criteria. Once these are decided, the phases of learning next identified reflect a model of the gradual instructional release. Although this model, as viewed in the template, shares the instructional path of beginning with modeling followed by guided practice, collaboration, and independence, the pathway is reciprocal (Grant et al., 2012) and can start with investigative collaboration, followed by modeling as needed as students move to independence. The goal of every lesson should be that your students gain the skills needed to ensure they are able to write for every situation in which they are asked to do so. You'll find completed lesson charts for each focus area of this book, along with useful tools for each lesson, in the Appendix.

It is our hope that all these tools, coupled with your professional expertise and knowledge of your students, will provide powerful classroom experiences that develop not only writing skills but thinking skills. We're

Figure 0.2 ◆ Points to Consider: Lesson Planning Template

Lesson Focus: ____

____

Standards Addressed (input the content standards you are addressing)

Purpose Statements (identify the learning intentions)

Success Criteria (identify what students will know and do to demonstrate success toward achieving the purpose statements)

Text Used and Rationale (list the texts used and indicate why you are using them)

Phase of Learning	Scaffolds/Supports
Show Me: Modeling/Direct Instruction **Share the purpose statements:** **Modeling/Think Aloud (script your think aloud for modeling)**	Indicate how you will support all learners in your class to understand the modeling.
Help Me: Guided Practice **Provide opportunities for students to try out the strategies you have modeled.**	Indicate how you will support all learners in your class to practice strategies. Include supports, like visuals, and note questions you will offer to prompt thinking.
Let Us: Collaboration Provide opportunities for students to discuss and share ideas and to work together productively.	Indicate how your students will work together to discuss and clarify their learning and note what they will plan and create together.
Let Me: Independent Provide opportunities for students to showcase their learning on their own.	Indicate how you will support students to show and/or demonstrate their learning.

inviting you on a shared journey to envision all that is known about purposeful and impactful writing as you think with us about how to enable students to be ready to use their arsenal of knowledge about best writing practices as they venture into any new writing situation with confidence.

PAUSE AND CONSIDER

Jot down a few goals you have in mind as you read this book. What do you hope to learn? Why?

____

____

____

____

____

Return to your "why" as you work through this book to help focus your reading.

CHAPTER ONE

Purpose
Why Am I Writing This?

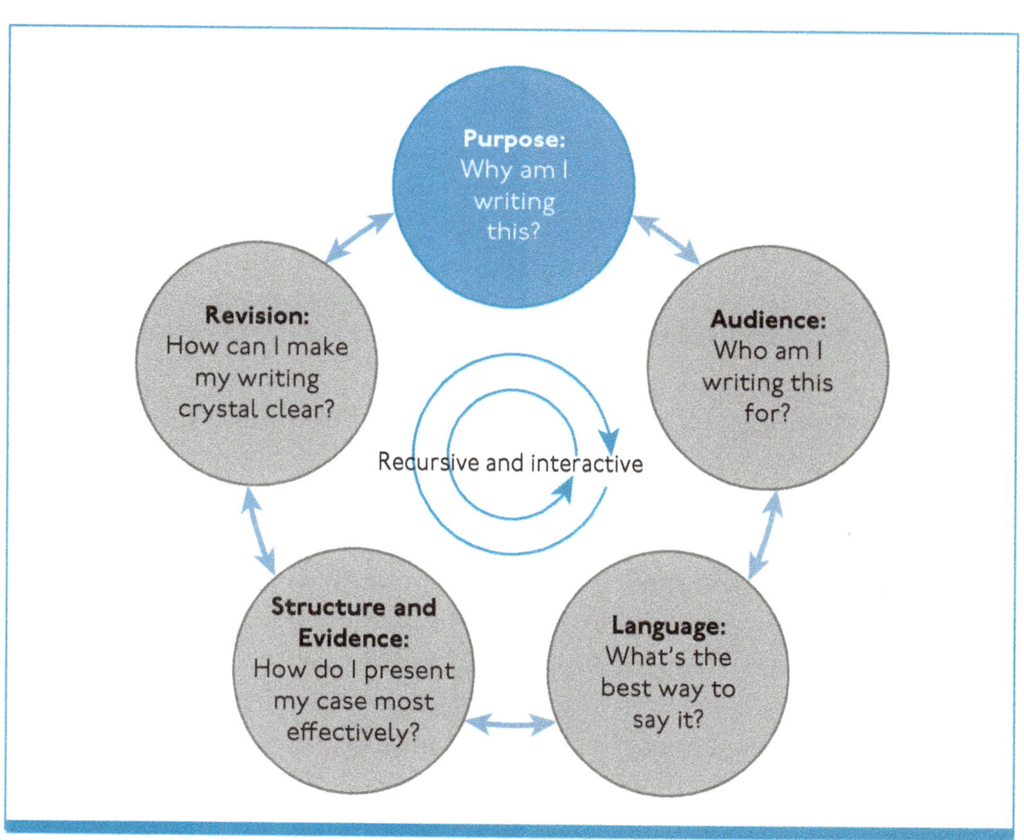

When I sit down to write a book, I do not say to myself, "I am going to produce a work of art." I write it because there is some lie that I want to expose, some fact to which I want to draw attention, and my initial concern is to get a hearing.

—George Orwell

ANTICIPATION GUIDE

The focus of this chapter is on **purpose**. Before reading this chapter, stop for a minute to complete the anticipation guide below to check your knowledge about the importance of establishing purpose when you're communicating. The three points you'll consider when reading the anticipation guide highlight the information we're sharing in this chapter. When you finish the chapter, you'll be able to revisit these three points in the chapter's Sum It Up section to self-assess what new information you've learned.

Anticipation Guide

Possible Fact	True	False
Knowing one's purpose helps to maintain a focus throughout any activity or writing.		
A clear statement of purpose informs the reader of what to anticipate in the text.		
Peer editing often confuses the focus of the purpose.		

"Why are we doing this?" This question rings in the ears of teachers as their students grapple with understanding the relevance of what they are learning or when they are asked to complete a specific task or learn some new information. This question is not only echoed by students; it's also often asked by teachers. We might find ourselves considering the *why* of our involvement when sitting in a rambling professional development session, during a meeting without clear objectives, or while participating in an activity with unconnected parts and tasks (e.g., trying to call into a customer service support line). We know that having a clear purpose is key to teaching our audiences of students and key to keeping them engaged, motivated, and willing to undertake the journey of learning. We like to think of purpose as the GPS app on our phones; it not only tells us how to get where we are going, but it considers our special circumstances or needs. In many classrooms purpose statements are shared with students before a lesson begins, referred to throughout the lesson, and revisited at the conclusion. Presenting a purpose for writing is no different—without it, our students may struggle with envisioning their end point and making the appropriate moves and choices to get there.

When a lesson or text is planned with a clear understanding of the intended outcome, the initiator, be it the teacher, student or writer, has a guideline to assess if progress is being made toward the anticipated purpose. (Wiggins & McTighe, 2005). In fact, as Fisher and Frey (2021) note, teachers who establish purpose report that both their focus and that of their students is increased and accomplished. Additionally, Hattie (2023) states that clarity of statements regarding purpose and intentions has an effect size of 0.85 because all elements of guessing are removed and the path to understanding and achievement is clear. Since an effect size of 0.40 equates to one year of growth in learning, teacher clarity has a tremendous impact on students, nearly doubling the rate of learning in a year.

The power of clarity is also important when written texts are shared. Both the author and the recipient must have no misgivings about the intent of the shared information. Clarity certainly eliminates or reduces any potential for miscommunication.

WHAT IS THE PURPOSE?

It's not uncommon to need support to clearly see the path to accomplishing our purpose. For example, Sheriff Elaine Tarantino recently visited friends in Barcelona, Spain, and wanted to explore the nearby beach town of Sitges. Her hosts recommended that she take the picturesque seaside roads instead of the most direct route (which would land her on efficient—but not scenic—highways) by selecting the "avoid highways" option on her GPS app. Sheriff Tarantino's friends knew what her purpose should be: to not only get to Sitges, but to also see certain landmarks along the way. Without this sense of purpose at the beginning, Sheriff Tarantino (and her app) would not have put her on the correct route, and she would have missed an integral part of her experience in Spain.

Purpose in writing functions in a similar way: without it, readers may find themselves on a route they didn't anticipate. At best, that route may be efficient but not appropriate for their needs. At worst, they may end with a wrong conclusion or pull out of the task completely. When preparing for a writing experience, students may also need support to identify their purpose and the path for accomplishing it, especially if the structure of writing they are attempting is unfamiliar to them. To prepare students to understand the importance of identifying their purpose for a writing task and then know how to proceed accordingly, we need to acquaint them with different types of purpose called for in real job situations. They need experiences that promote the idea that they will be called upon to complete various types of writing tasks in any career they choose. Knowing the

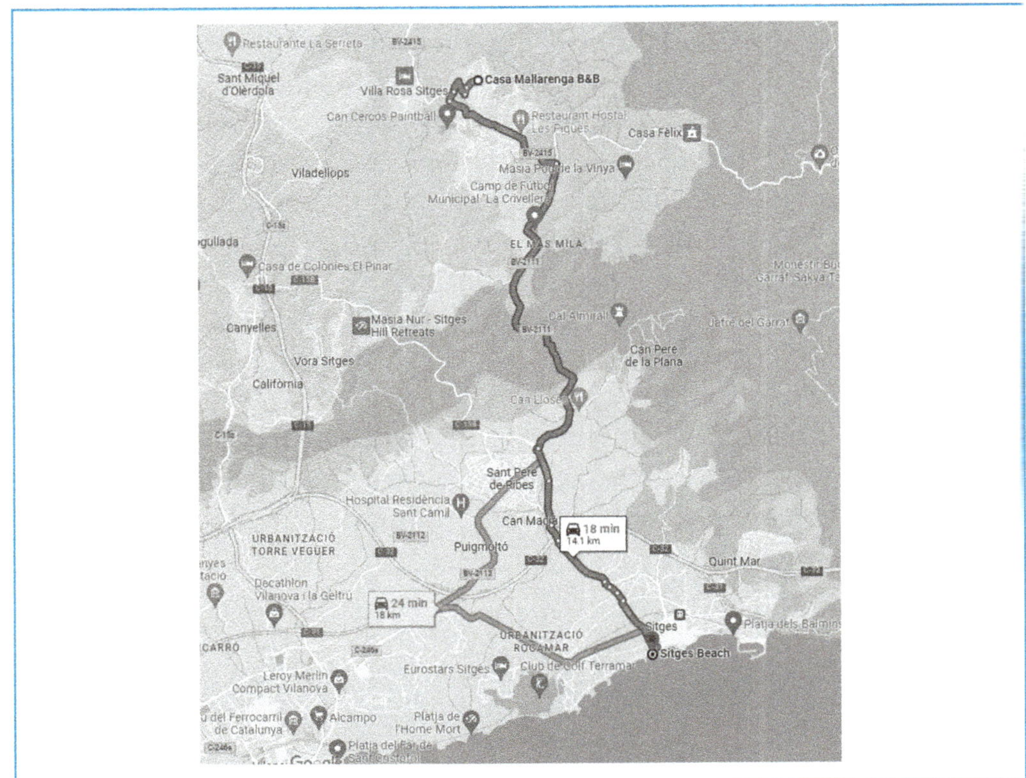

purpose of their writing and then being able to create an appropriate plan will promote success with their lifelong writing endeavors.

The Different Types of Writing Purposes

Perhaps the best-known teacher of purpose is Aristotle, who identified three modes of persuasion that are often referenced by English teachers: to teach, to inform, and to delight. While most reasons for writing do fit into these three modes, expanding them a bit provides more possibility regarding the intentions of writers, especially as they move into workplace situations. We've attempted this expansion between writing in the classroom and writing beyond the classroom by building, through example, beyond Gallagher's (2011) "6 Real-World Writing Purposes" which he developed from the work of Bean et al. (2003) (see Figure 1.1). We have expanded the explanation of the role the writer plays in the writing situation and have also provided examples to show where this writing exists in the workplace.

Figure 1.1 • Six Main Writing Purposes

Purpose	Explanation	Examples
Express and Reflect	The writer . . . . . . describes something from his or her own experience. . . . uses that experience to reflect on who he or she is as a person; reflects on how he or she fits in the world; and/or reflects on broader questions about culture, humanity, and the planet.	Blog Memoir Editorial Poetry Fiction/nonfiction
Inform and Explain	The writer . . . . . . tells the reader about something (or someone) he or she didn't know about before or gives new information about someone (or something) the reader already knows about.	News article Report Presentation Incident report
Evaluate and Judge	The writer . . . . . . "reviews" something (could be a restaurant, song, sports team, YouTube video, brand of cell phone, etc.). . . . may compare two or more things.	Critique Review Evaluation Financial review Consumer report Product reviews
Inquire and Explore	The writer . . . . . . takes on an open-ended question or problem. . . . explores it and "wrestles with it" during the course of the piece.	Research project Proposal Article/blog Arts review
Analyze and Interpret	The writer . . . . . . examines a scientific study, piece of data, movie, poem, meme, etc., and analyzes its form and content, thereby revealing interesting things about both the piece under analysis and the wider world.	Data analysis Art review White paper
Take a Stand/ Propose a Solution	The writer . . . . . . makes an argument about something that matters to him or her. . . . may be writing in order to propose a specific solution, or simply to expose a problem.	Opinion-editorial Speech Persuasive essay Social media campaign Infographic

YOUR TURN: MAKING A MODEL TEXT

Now using what was learned from the experience of Sheriff Tarantino and her friends and also the six main writing purposes shared in Figure 1.1, write a website post to your students that makes obvious your purpose for writing. Using the template in Figure 1.2 you might inquire about their opinion regarding your school's cell phone policy or inform them of your instructional plan for the semester, or inquire about topics they would like to have explored or ask their opinion regarding a possible text they would like to have added to the curriculum. Once you select the topic make the purpose for writing explicit. The template below is similar to the one you'll ask students to use when they do this activity themselves.

Figure 1.2 • Web Post Writing Template

Purpose:
Audience:
Online Post:

Self-assessment check:

- Addresses my audience with an appropriate greeting.
- Expresses the **intent/purpose** early in the body of the communication.
- Uses language that strikes a friendly yet professional tone.
- Messaging is clear, understandable, and approachable.
- Closes using professional words and in the way you want to be addressed.
- Contains signature (if needed) and contact information (if needed).

THEIR TURN: WRITING USING MODELS

After a think-aloud identifying how you made your writing choices in your website post to students, invite them to use your example as a model to craft a message to an audience they choose. Again, emphasize how you addressed the **purpose** in your message and invite students to also identify the **purpose** for writing in their message. When they finish, invite them to self-assess their message to determine if it

- contains a greeting,

- expresses the **intent/purpose** early in the body of the communication,

- uses language that strikes an appropriate tone,

- contains clear, understandable, and approachable language, and

- closes appropriately with contact information and their signature (if needed).

Have them revise and edit accordingly. This would be a perfect opportunity to invite students to share their paragraphs with a peer(s) and also to coedit each other's text.

Students can use the downloadable graphic organizer, Student Writing Template, found at resources.corwin.com/ClassroomToCareer.

WHY SHOULD WE FOCUS ON UNDERSTANDING PURPOSE?

You may be thinking that many of the purposes of writing in Figure 1.1 seem very "English-y," but throughout this book, we hope to demonstrate how many careers, especially those that don't seem writing heavy on the surface, require writing tasks involving at least one of the six identified purposes. Writing is a component of most jobs. In fact, *Forbes* magazine noted that most financially lucrative jobs like technical writers and editors, engineers, traditional journalists, nurses, editorial directors, editors-in-chief, web developers, and carpenters need accurate spelling, grammar, and punctuation skills to be able communicate ideas clearly and succinctly with employers, clients, and supervisors (Anders, 2016). Writing skills are also prevalent in newer careers that involve sharing digital content through writing. So if you're preparing content strategists, content marketing managers, content managers, nurses, engineers, and web producers, carpenters, and, yes, even plumbers who track expenses, take inventory, order supplies, and plan project calendars, they'll need to know how to write. There are also careers within business development, science technical writing, and policy analysis that require writing for a purpose. What all these careers have in common is the need for capable, confident writers who know they

- are writing to an identified audience,

- want to share a particular message (**purpose**),

- want to say it the best way possible,

- want to use a language style that will be received well, and

- want to include information that will accomplish their goal.

Yes, folks with English degrees aren't the only people who need to be confident in their writing skills. The majority of professions require some knowledge of writing and the purpose of each written text must be clear if its author is to be successful in sharing information. Consider that most people in the workforce are similar to Sheriff Tarantino. She uses writing daily in her position, providing police reports for incidents and daily routines. It is hard to find a job today that doesn't require strong writing skills.

HOW DO WE SUPPORT STUDENTS TO THINK ABOUT PURPOSE WHEN THEY WRITE?

If you aren't yet convinced that writing will play a major role in almost any career, consider the national content teaching standards. Why do they all specifically emphasize the importance of purposeful writing? The answer is probably because writing will play a part in every career choice. Take a close look at standards for purpose-based writing from the Common Core English Language Arts, the root of many state standards throughout the United States. While standards may differ slightly across state lines, teachers in every state will be able to call out standards that connect writing and purpose. Most standards, regardless of discipline, highlight purposeful writing. For example,

- World history standards call for writers to use words, phrases, and clauses to link the major sections of the text, create cohesion, and clarify the relationships between claim(s) and reasons, between reasons and evidence, and between claim(s) and counterclaims (CCSS.ELA-Literacy.WHST.9-10.1c).

- Math standards highlight a focus on purpose as they ask writers to describe the nature of the attribute under investigation, including how it was measured and its units of measurement (CCSS.MATH. CONTENT.6.SP.B.5.B).

- Similar to these, the Next Generation Science standards ask writers to obtain, evaluate, and communicate their intent or purpose for sharing information (NGSS).

Notice in these standards students are called upon to engage the audience with a clear statement of their intent or purpose.

As you were reading each of these content standards that focused on the development of writing skills for students, you probably realized that regardless of one's profession the creators of these standards feel that one must be taught to be a competent writer because there will be a need to share information in some type of written form. Students must be prepared to write in any profession since having writing skills is at the top of the list of what employers look for when interviewing and hiring in most professions, notes Burning Glass Technologies—a software company that identifies employment trends by mining employment ads to cull employment trends and requisites for employment. It's clear that being able to share information in writing can win a person the employment opportunity.

In all of the career examples you will see throughout this book, we present how real people navigate the demands of their workplace by knowing how to use writing to communicate using their institutions' common language and values to achieve a shared purpose. Linguist Swales (1988) termed this phenomena a "discourse community" and described them as "groups that have goals and purposes, and use communication to achieve their goals." Students, often unknowingly, are also members of many discourse communities but need us to help them understand what that means, and how to leverage their membership to their advantage. Examples of common non-career discourse communities could include families, members of a fraternity or sorority, contributors to the same academic journal, or fan club members who post to a shared blog for their favorite artist.

As seasoned members of multiple discourse communities where we share many variations of language from very informal to very formal, we know that writing efforts are a fruitless endeavor if they lack a sense of purpose. When reflecting on your own tools for purposeful writing, you would most likely find a wide base of model texts living in your brains. Ones that you use to guide your writing. For example, an English teacher knows the overall purpose and components of a successful argument quite well, whereas a history buff will have deep knowledge of the characteristics of a government document that guides its purpose as an informational text, and a sports enthusiast or broadcaster will know how to compile and purposefully share data in the form of newscasts and events.

PAUSE AND CONSIDER

What discourse communities do you participate in? How about your students? Think about intersections and differences and how these affect your verbal and written communication. As you read through the book and examples, return and jot down any new ideas you have.

____

____

____

____

____

Because we each participate in multiple discourse communities, we can select which text style is best to use, when to use a particular one, and why to use it. For example, a banker writing an email to her client might choose to send graphs and diagrams to explain interest rates for a mortgage loan, and then would also add other clarifying text if she knows more information is needed to promote the message. She may add a description shared in words or an additional illustration. This would occur because her purpose is to convey information to her targeted audience and to do so she must consider both her intent and the base of knowledge of her audience. These behaviors can be taught and continually refined through instructional opportunities that invite writers to reconceptualize how to share information by considering their purpose and their audience. (Chapter 2 digs deeper into determining audience need.)

To begin teaching students the power of having a clear purpose for their writing, explain how they must ask themselves _what's my reason or purpose for writing this text? What is my intent for this written communication?_ Remind them not to confuse the topic of their writing with the purpose for their writing.

Encourage them to identify their purpose for writing by considering:

Am I writing this particular piece to do one or more of the following?

- Inform the reader regarding information or a position
- Share a personal account
- Share data or entertain
- Critique or offer a review
- Argue a position
- Compile notes about a study, data, or a text
- Propose a solution
- State or expose a problem
- Ask for help
- Explore a concept or idea
- Offer help or consultation

Without being redundant, it's important to identify that the purpose for writing is a major step to sharing the message. Sharing models can help your students understand how other writers have shared their purpose in the texts they write. Much like a fledgling musician emulates (and even copies) his or her musical heroes, a developing writer might gain a sense of what good writing is—and then begin to imitate it—by seeing excellent examples. In order to facilitate this transfer from mimic to master, teachers must offer students opportunities to dissect and understand how effective texts approach audience, promote a purpose, and are never finished on the first draft.

YOUR TURN: THINK-ALOUD

To begin, model for students how you would peruse many texts related to the topic you plan to write about. Encourage students to note how each author established the purpose for their writing. Point out several. Then select a text and script a think-aloud to show students how you would identify the author's purpose of a text related to a topic of interest to you. Also illustrate how you would note evidence supportive of your thinking. To illustrate this thinking-aloud process, we'll share an example with a biology focus.

(Continued)

(Continued)

Notice in this example of an article from the Centers for Disease Control and Prevention (CDC), shown as Figure 1.3, how scientific evidence is used for the purpose of spurring an audience to action. Use the graphic organizer in Figure 1.4 and annotations to analyze and track how an author establishes purpose within a text. Further model for students by reading the CDC's feature on environmental health (available online at https://www.atsdr.cdc.gov/features/toxicsubstances/index.html). Next evaluate how it sets a purpose and then uses evidence and reasoning to support its aim of informing a wide audience about toxic substances. Ultimately, the goal is for students to develop a schema for writing once they have identified their purpose.

Figure 1.3 • This CDC Website Has a Purpose

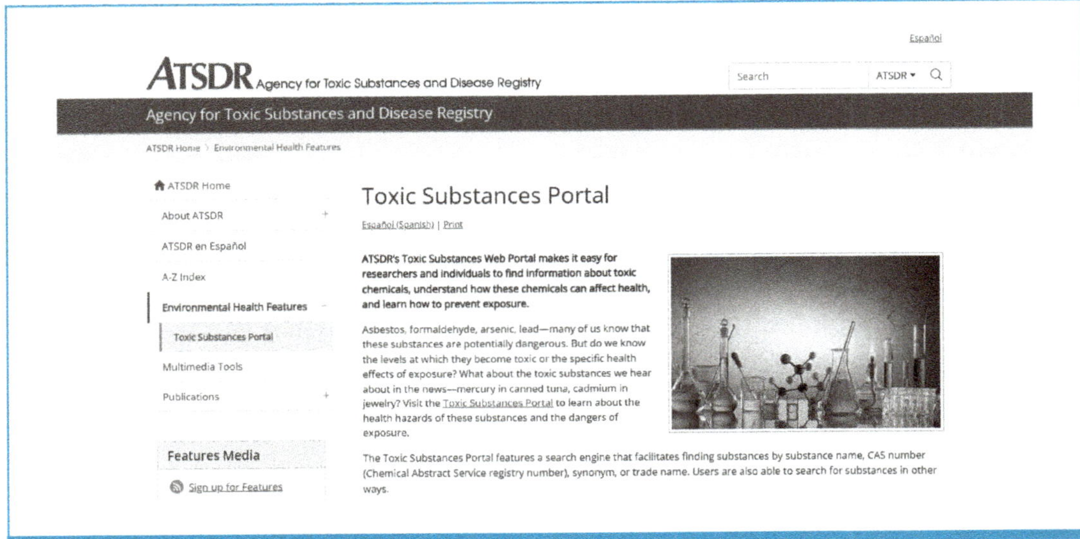

Source: Agency for Toxic Substances and Disease Registry/Center for Disease Control.

Figure 1.4 • Purpose/Evidence Graphic Organizer—Part 1

Purpose of text: *To inform the reader*	Textual evidence (where did you find the purpose?): *"ATSDR's Toxic Substances Web Portal makes it easy for researchers and individuals to find information about toxic chemicals...." —The author is sharing an informational website that will be a learning resource for those that explore it. The author is informing the readers that this resource exists for their use.*

THEIR TURN: STUDENT PRACTICE

Now offer students a more complex text that presents data and action steps. Choose a text that corresponds to a topic you are teaching. We'll share an example of how this might work with an article from the online source Science Daily. Our example text, *Uncertainty on climate change in textbooks linked to uncertainty in students* (North Carolina State University, 2021, see https://bit.ly/3Yqdk2l), is a summation of a longer research article. Intended for an audience with a deeper science background, students could alternatively read the original article that this summative Science Daily article is based on (Busch, 2021, *Textbooks of doubt, tested: the effect of a denialist framing on adolescents' certainty about climate change*).

Ask students to identify the purpose in the text and record their insights in the Tracking Purpose in a Text graphic organizer (Figure 1.5; downloadable from the companion website). Always model, using a think-aloud, how you would use the graphic organizer. For example, you can think aloud about the first few lines in the Science Daily article noted above like this:

Access this Science Daily article via the QR code (bit.ly URL in above paragraph)

The first sentence of the article states, "A new study from North Carolina State University suggests textbook wording that portrays climate change information as uncertain can influence how middle and high school students feel about the information, even for students who say they already know about climate change and its human causes." I think this is clarifying the purpose of this article which is to inform readers that textbooks can affect how students think about a science topic—climate change in particular. I think they are going to cite data to support this claim. I'm going to make a note in the graphic organizer to document what I notice in the text about purpose.

Figure 1.5 • Purpose/Evidence Graphic Organizer Example

Article: Uncertainty on climate change in textbooks linked to uncertainty in students, from Science Daily online (https://bit.ly/3Yqdk2l)

Purpose of text	Textual evidence (where did you find the purpose?):
Example: to inform the reader that textbook wording affects the student-reader.	*Example: A new study from North Carolina State University suggests textbook wording that portrays climate change information as uncertain can influence how middle and high school students feel about the information, even for students who say they already know about climate change and its human causes.*

(Continued)

(Continued)

Purpose of text	Textual evidence (provide evidence of the strategy):
Example: to inform the reader that students' prior knowledge of climate change had little effect on their thinking as they read a text about climate change.	*Busch saw that knowledge and beliefs of students and of the people in their social circle didn't have a statistically significant impact on how students reacted to the textbook information.*
Purpose of text *To inform the public that some textbooks are not up to date in terms of climate change information.*	Textual evidence (provide evidence of the strategy): *Busch said that there are other signs that climate change topics are absent or mistreated in classrooms. A report from the National Center for Science Education found 10 states received a grade of D or worse for their standards for climate change education, and that included some of the country's most populous states.*
Purpose of text *To inform readers that there are other influences on students' understandings of climate change.*	Textual evidence (provide evidence of the strategy): *Other studies have found that social norms — such as the beliefs and attitudes of their friends and family members — can be very influential for teens and can predict how accepting young people are of climate change.*

online resources

It's important to remind students that the purpose for writing will vary across disciplines and across careers. There are several examples shared below, but when looking for your own models to share with students, be sure to find ones that make each purpose obvious to readers. Share models or even create examples to illustrate how writers think through the purpose for their message. The models you select should exhibit the features you want students to see and emulate. These include:

- **Make it specific.** Your statement of purpose should tell the reader exactly why you are writing. For example, Are you writing to express something, to inform the reader, to persuade the reader, or to share a work you've created?

- **Make it clear.** After reading your purpose, none should wonder about your intent.

- **Make it concise.** Get to the point quickly; add supports as needed.

- **Make it obvious.** Your topical expertise should be obvious.

- **Make it succinct.** Say it once; avoid repeating.

PAUSE AND CONSIDER

What are the most common purposes for writing in your discipline? What specifically will you look for in the model texts you choose? Which specific standards would you like to focus on? Note any specific models you might use from this book as you read through the chapters.

____

____

____

____

____

The following examples can be shared with students to emphasize how purpose matters in several careers with varied disciplinary backgrounds:

1. As a landscaper, I am writing to a client (audience). I aim to share the scope of work I intend to get a contract for. The reaction I want to achieve is that the client understands what I will do during this project, they think my rate is fair for the scope of work, and they hire me. My purpose for writing this piece is to **persuade** the customer that I am the perfect person for the job.

2. Regardless of one's work position, adults often have a need to share their thinking in a letter to a company or political figure. I am incensed about the increase in gas prices, so I am writing a letter to the editor of the local paper (audience). My purpose is **to take a stand** and **explain** why I think our gas tax should be revoked and also **inquire** if others want to join me in writing a petition to the governor.

3. I am having a conflict with a coworker because of misunderstandings about our responsibilities. I want to accomplish two purposes with my message: I want to **inform** my employer (audience) of the problem and **express** my willingness to meet with the employer and colleague to identify a solution to resolve the problem.

4. I have analyzed a section of a scientific reading with the purpose of **explaining** some specific information to peers (audience) I am working with in a collaborative writing group.

5. I want to **inform** the owner of the local art gallery (audience) that I would like to share my portfolio for her review. My purpose is to **showcase my work** with the intent of having it displayed in the gallery.

Once you've shared models from your discipline, offer students a sentence frame to support them in identifying the reason, the purpose for their writing.

THEIR TURN: IDENTIFYING AUDIENCE AND PURPOSE

SENTENCE FRAME SUPPORT

I am writing this piece to share with _____ (audience) _____________. The reaction I am hoping to achieve from this audience is _____________. My purpose for writing this piece is to _____________.

Note to self: Do I have all of the facts and language I need to write this piece now, or do I need to investigate some information in order to achieve my goal or purpose?

Note, too, that purpose and audience walk hand in hand. Chapter 2 provides further support in teaching students how to consider audience in their writing.

Once students have established a purpose for their writing, invite them to share their examples in small groups and have their peers respond by telling them if they understand the reason they are writing and also if the response they are hoping to obtain is clear.

Composing for a Specific Purpose

Before students begin composing, guide them to build an understanding of a topic and to identify their purpose for writing. There are several ways to give students practice writing with purpose in mind, but here we'll continue with an example from a science class, to build on the model texts described previously. Science teachers might guide students to **investigate a science-based issue that impacts lives,** such as:

- clean drinking water,

- national parks protection,

- single use plastics,

- carbon-based fuels,

- ocean acidification, and others.

Ask students to investigate an issue they choose by reviewing research and data around their topic.

Collaborative conversations among students researching the same, or related topics, can also help them to develop deeper understandings around the topic. Consider asking students to discuss these questions: What's the issue? What data surrounds the issue? What are the various opinions around the issue? What are the implications for people, society, and/or future studies? What are the important details to share with others? What are the concerns?

Students will need to consider credible sources when studying their topics. If they need help evaluating source credibility, this article by Lapp et al. (2014) identifies criteria for credible source selection. Scan the QR code to access this article.

https://bit.ly/4ISIHUh

Have students write letters to a local government agency, a community board, or some other entity that has the ability and authority to act on the issue. Students should include data, research-based ideas, and they should clearly convey their desire for action and/or change.

THEIR TURN: CLARIFYING PURPOSE IN DRAFTS

After students have a "first go" at their writing, have them review their message to be sure their purpose is clear. If not, the following questions can support adding additional clarity. Use these feedback stems to help students home in on the reason for writing while keeping the intended audience in mind.

- I'm noticing that many of our letters have effective (scientific) evidence about _______________ and examples of how you see _______________ affecting our environment/lives; however, I don't get a sense of what you want me to do with that information. What could you add to clarify this?

- What do you want the board/organization/person to do?

- Why do you want him/her/they to act?

(Continued)

(Continued)

- How could the reader(s) of this text make a difference?

- What role could you play in further action?

- What next steps could you outline?

- You have a plan/ideas for action. What else could you add to emphasize the purpose of this writing?

- What needs to stop to further a positive outcome?

- Consider adding this: We request the following three [four, five, etc.] measures be implemented by the _______________: [list continues here]

After students review a few model texts and identify the purpose for which each has written, have them revisit their own writing. Science texts can be found easily via a web search. Here are a few places to start:

- Time for Kids/Science: https://www.timeforkids.com/g56/sections/science/

- Science Daily: https://www.sciencedaily.com/

- National Geographic Kids: https://kids.nationalgeographic.com/

- Science News: https://www.sciencenews.org/

Single-Point Rubric to Guide Writing

Provide a rubric to help students determine if their piece of writing needs more revision or editing. We prefer a single-point rubric such as the one in Figure 1.6 because it focuses on the expected level of proficiency. In forthcoming chapters, we'll discuss aspects of writing beyond purpose including audience, voice, evidence, and revision. For now, the rubric in this figure focuses on how purpose might connect to these other aspects of writing. (You can download this rubric from the online companion as well.)

Figure 1.6 • Purpose-driven Writing Rubric

Needs Work	Meets Expectations	Exceeds expectations
	My piece has a clear, locatable purpose and message. It can be summarized in a sentence or two. I have demonstrated knowledge of my audience by: • My word choice (I have used language that is appropriate to my audience). • My use of evidence (I have included examples, illustrations, and other artifacts that will best convince my audience). • My tone (I have made certain stylistic choices to further my purpose with my audience). • My formatting choices (I have considered the structure that best suits my purpose and audience). I have used outside, credible sources to support my thinking. I have used the editing and revision process to refine and tighten my work; there is evidence of change between my first and last drafts. I have solicited feedback from a non-classmate and included a feedback form.	

As seen in this example, the single-point rubric helps students identify areas that need more work and areas that exceed criteria. The rubric is specific and detailed in terms of criteria. A teacher can add notes to the rubric, if desired. Single-point rubrics are clear, easy to read, and provide an opportunity for students to reflect on their work, receive feedback, and can then be used to guide revisions. We find that it makes the success criteria obvious to the student. Single-point rubrics have a few advantages worth considering:

• they take much less time to create than, say, an analytical one;

• students are more likely to read and use them because they are less wordy; and

• they place fewer limits on the potential of the assignment.

Revision based on feedback.

The writing process is not complete until the writer has revised based on feedback offered by the teacher or a peer. We'll discuss feedback and editing in greater detail in a forthcoming chapter and will just touch on the processes here as they relate to purpose. The peer feedback process offers a benefit for the reviewer and for the reviewee. A peer feedback form offers a structure that guides the reviewer to focus on key areas (Figure 1.7; downloadable from online companion). Peers focus on the intended purpose, given the audience which is identified by the writer of the text. Students should use the feedback to fine-tune their writing.

Figure 1.7 • Purposeful Writing Feedback Form

Writer Name: ____

Reviewer Name: ____

<table>
<tr><td colspan="1">Writer fills in this section:

Purpose for writing (what do you want the reader to think or believe?):

____

____</td></tr>
<tr><td>Who is your audience?

____

____</td></tr>
<tr><td>Reviewer fills in this section:

Purpose for writing (What do you identify as the purpose of this writing? Cite your evidence.)

____

____

____</td></tr>
<tr><td>Is the writing appropriate for the audience? (Explain your response.)

____

____

____</td></tr>
<tr><td>Do you have any other comments or suggestions for the writer?

____

____

____</td></tr>
</table>

Success Criteria Checklist.

The final step is for students to evaluate their learning against the earlier established success criteria. Figure 1.8 shows a success criteria checklist that students could use to note their own growth.

Figure 1.8 • Success Criteria Checklist

- I located and underlined my thesis sentence[s] that indicate the purpose of my text.
- I reverse-outlined my paragraphs; each paragraph makes a single point to support my purpose.
- I found and circled my evidence; it directly supports and is appropriate for my purpose.
- I provide reasoning to explain my evidence; I have highlighted my reasoning.
- My writing (Op-Ed) has been read by another person and I have used the peer feedback to revise.

SUM IT UP

As we guide our students along their journey of becoming confident readers and writers, we must not forget the importance of a plan. Just as we make a list before we go to the grocery store or—like our first example with Sheriff Tarantino—plan a route for a road trip before we go, the writing our students do needs to have a clear focus and trajectory. As we hope you've seen in this chapter, competent, purposeful writing begins with identifying the purpose for writing and then examining models to clarify the intent. There should be little mystery about how or why a model text has achieved its purpose; too often students are excluded from understanding the inner workings of a text. Let's pull back the curtain and give them the tools they need to analyze good writing. When students know how successful writing works, they are more likely to produce it themselves!

ANTICIPATION GUIDE

Revisit the anticipation guide that appeared at the beginning of the chapter to check and expand your initial responses. Even if you had the correct answer, now you can add an explanation that illustrates your deepened understanding.

Possible Fact	True	False	What else can you add?
Knowing one's purpose helps to maintain a focus throughout any activity or writing.	T		
A clear statement of purpose informs the reader of what to anticipate in the text.	T		
Peer editing often confuses the focus of the purpose.		F	Peer editing is an additional support to writers that often helps them to identify how well the purpose of their text is being understood.

CHAPTER TWO

Audience
Who Am I Writing This For?

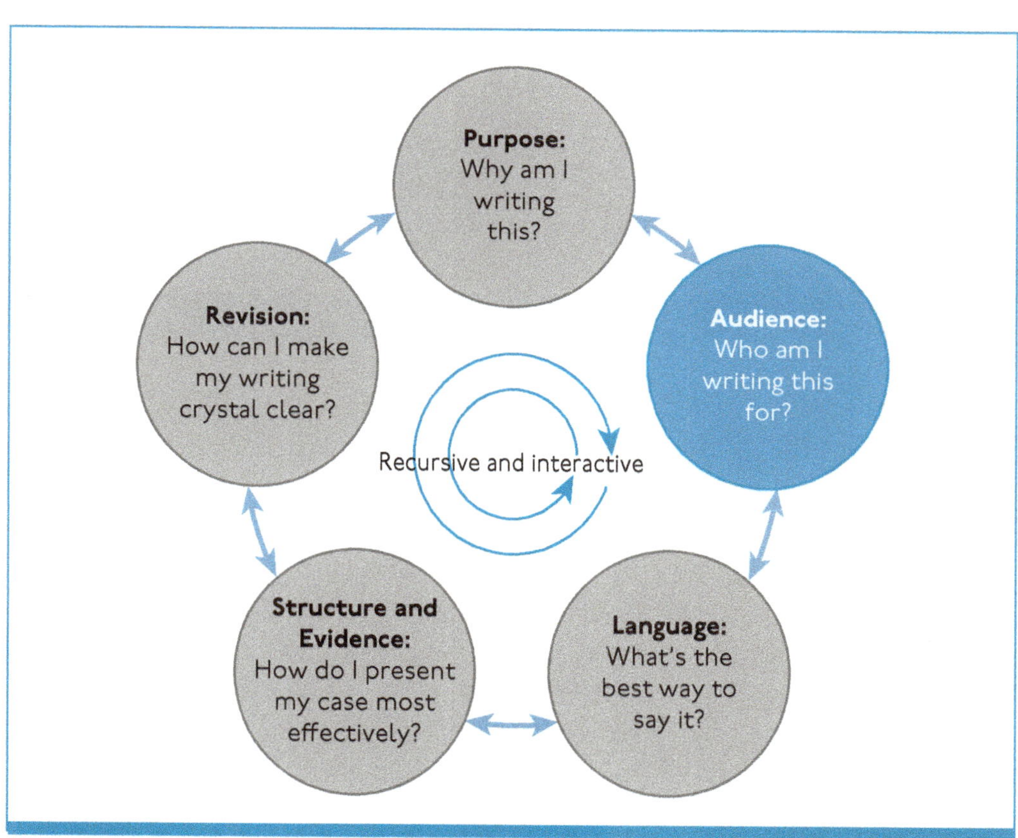

Your purpose is to make your audience see what you saw, hear what you heard, feel what you felt. Relevant detail, couched in concrete, colorful language, is the best way to recreate the incident as it happened and to picture it for the audience.

—Dale Carnegie

ANTICIPATION GUIDE

The focus of this chapter is on clarifying the **audience** to whom one is writing. Before reading this chapter, stop for a minute to complete the anticipation guide below to check your knowledge regarding the importance of understanding and addressing your audience when communicating. The three points you'll consider when reading the anticipation guide highlight the information shared in this chapter. When you finish reading, you'll be able to revisit these three points in the chapter's Sum It Up section to self-assess what new information you've learned.

Anticipation Guide

Possible Fact	True	False
When writing a message, regardless of the audience, the same tone, style, and structure must be used.		
Code-switching is appropriate depending on the audience.		
Most professions require writing, except for professions involving math.		

Imagine that you've just planted your first rose garden. While you don't yet understand the processes of feeding, pruning, and caring for roses, you've heard from your more expert friend that it's important to offer proper care, so that roses continue to grow and thrive. Your friend shares an article that he just read about feeding, training vines, and other detailed information that even has what seems like the chemistry of feeding roses included. While you appreciate the kind offering of an article, you realize that as a novice, you need a different kind of article—something that offers step-by-step, easy-to-follow guidance, labeled diagrams, and definitions of terminology, so that you can learn about canes, secateurs, and outward facing buds. To gain this understanding you decide to search for an article that better fits you as a novice reader. The articles you find are quite different. The one written for the novice is much less detailed and assumes an entry level base of knowledge. For example, the article for a novice might read, *"It's important to water your rose vines deeply and regularly especially during the hot summer months."* In comparison, an article written to an expert might read,

> Watering is crucial for the health of your rose bushes. Just a reminder, it's important to water the roots, not the leaves, deeply because getting the leaves wet can promote disease. A good rule of thumb to remember is to water your roses once or twice a week depending on weather. Once your plants are well-established, the watering needs depend on the soil conditions. Certain soils, like adobe or heavy clay, retain moisture. With such, solid, weekly watering may be sufficient. Loamy soils may need more watering since these soils don't retain water. You will have to observe the soil to establish your own watering pattern.

Did you notice that much more detail is contained in the article intended for the expert because the author assumes a more extensive base of knowledge, which includes experience and language? When writing to an audience of novices, the author may decide that the information should be less detailed because the novice has a much shallower base of topical knowledge.

As readers, we learn best when the text we are reading is appropriate for our knowledge and experience. We become more engaged when the text fits our needs and targets our interests. But how does a writer know how to best address their readers? One of the best ways to accomplish this is to consider various aspects of the target audience. According to Land (2022), "Rather than learning forms or conventions of writing for the sake of learning them, writers who consider purpose and audience in their work are grounded in the sociocultural nature of writing; they write to do things in the world." We see this as empowering and motivating. When writing is authentic and audience focused, it has the potential to impact, influence, and affect change. When writing is driven by personal, social, community, or work needs, it can help the author to accomplish aims.

Consider all the ways you and others you know communicate on a professional level. Today's world offers many ways to connect with our audiences of coworkers, colleagues, and associates. We might be emailing, blogging, composing news articles, posting in social media, video blogging, creating schematics, diagramming, or illustrating. There are a multitude of ways that people communicate daily and also in work environments, and there is a style, tone, and structure for each message. The language, however, changes depending on what the author knows about the audience intended for the message.

PAUSE AND CONSIDER

Do you think technology has enhanced or limited your power of communication? Perhaps you think it has done both. Jot a few of your thoughts here and then revisit them as you share the ideas we've included in this chapter.

____

____

____

____

____

WHAT IS AUDIENCE?

Let's define *audience* and dig in to types of audiences. The audience is the group of people, or the person, for whom the author is composing. There are different types of audiences and some audiences are combinations of types. Audiences may be *experts, novices, technicians, decision-makers,* or a mix of these. Some audiences will fall into gray areas because of the mix of people included or they will exist beyond the boundaries of these categories since these categories do not represent all audience types. Despite this, it's helpful to consider these four audience types when beginning to craft your writing (see Figure 2.1).

Figure 2.1 • Audience Types and Characteristics

Type of Audience	Characteristics of Audience
Experts	have background knowledge, language, and insights that allow for depth in terms of written information.
Novices	are learning about the topic being written. They benefit from explanations, definitions, and other clarifying information that helps them grow in their understanding. Other features that may determine if a person is a novice are age, grade, and knowledge of the topical language.
Technicians	are often interested in applications, step-by-step guidelines, precautions, recommendations, and graphics, like flow charts.
Decision-makers	may be overseeing projects, plans, products, or efforts. They look for credibility, evidence, benefits, and methods of implementation.

While these categories will help a writer start to think about crafting strategically for their readers, often writing is for multiple audiences. What's most important is that the writer considers who their audience is and what the audience will be hoping to gain from their writing. Once identified it's important to know how to communicate effectively with that audience. A helpful starting point is to look at existing, authentic models that address a particular audience. For example, think about your workplace communications. Your audiences include parents, fellow teachers, and administrators. You know your audience and you often share brief messages with them via email. Your messages to parents are probably similar to those of 7th grade teacher Mike Seguro (Figure 2.2). The tone is courteous and informative as Mike expresses concern for a student, offers praise on an accomplishment, and just checks in. He certainly knows the format and his tone and style may be altered slightly because of his familiarity with the parents, who are his audience. Mike starts with a greeting, moves to the body paragraph where he expresses his intent for the message, closes with his contact information, and adds his signature which includes his name, title, and the name of the school. His paragraphs are like those of a formal letter. His language is professional but befitting of his target audience—parents who might not know all the jargon that he uses with his teacher colleagues. He makes sure his messaging is clear, understandable, and approachable. Mr. Seguro knows his audience of parents and composes a message that will effectively communicate his intentions. In the exercises that follow, you're asked to draft a sample letter to a specific audience (parents of your students), then you will use your letter as a model for students as they draft a letter to a specific audience of their choice.

Figure 2.2 • Mike Seguro's Letter to Parents

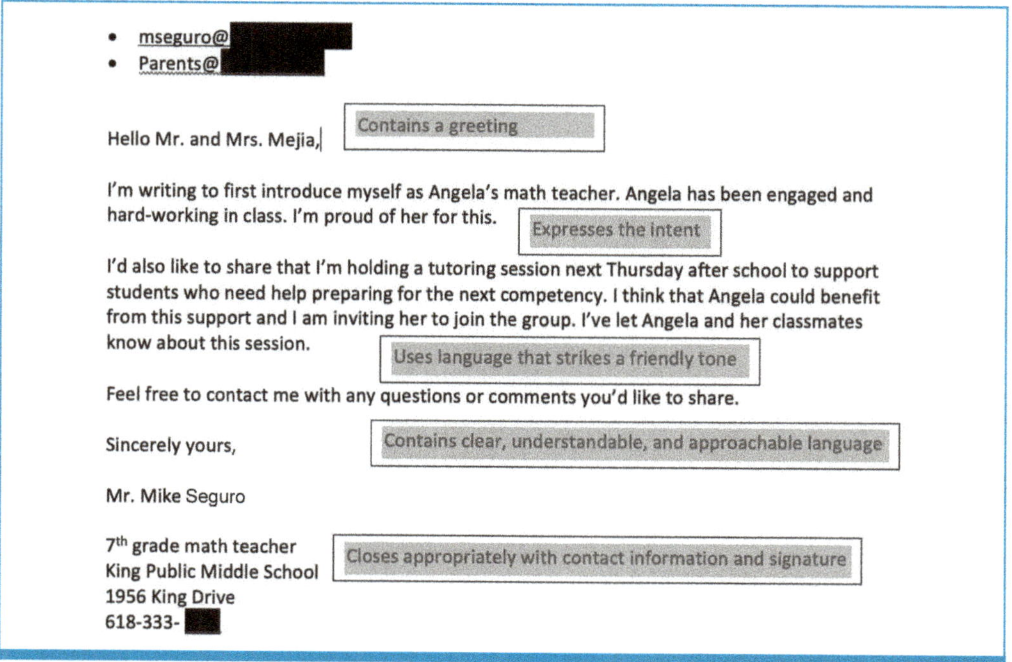

YOUR TURN: MODELING WRITING FOR AN AUDIENCE

Now using Mr. Seguro's example as a model, write a friendly but professional email to parents. Think about their strengths and needs. They probably fall within the range of novice to expert depending on the information you are about to share. Think about something you want to share; this is your purpose for writing. Is it to tell them something their child is doing well, or something they need help with, or to alert them to a meeting time to talk about their child, or something else? You decide the purpose for the audience you have identified and then craft your message. When you finish, self-assess to be sure you have included the elements shared by Mr. Seguro.

Purpose:
Audience:
Email:

Self-assessment check:

- Addresses my **audience** with an appropriate greeting.
- Expresses the intent early in the body of the letter.
- Uses language that strikes a friendly yet professional tone.
- Messaging is clear, understandable, and approachable.
- Closes using professional words and in the way you want to be addressed.
- Contains signature and contact information.

THEIR TURN: WRITING USING MODELS

After a think-aloud demonstrating how you made the writing choices that you made in your letter, invite students to use your letter or Mike Seguro's, which is labeled in Figure 2.2, as a model to craft a letter to an audience they choose. (Students can use the downloadable graphic organizer, Student Letter Template, found at resources.corwin .com/ClassroomToCareer.)

They should also identify their purpose for writing the message. When they finish, invite them to self-assess their message to determine if it

- contains a greeting,

- expresses the intent early in the body of the letter,

- uses language that strikes an appropriate tone,

- contains clear, understandable, and approachable language, and

- closes appropriately with contact information and their signature.

Have them revise and edit accordingly.

WHY SHOULD WE FOCUS ON UNDERSTANDING AUDIENCE?

Like Mike Seguro, Antoinette Brown who is an architect working for a design firm communicates in strategic, focused ways with a specific audience. When she connects with clients who comprise her audience population, she often presents schematics and annotated diagrams that best convey her message, along with a written accompaniment that adds detail to the diagrammatic plan. She knows that her audience, her intended readers, will have a range of knowledge in terms of reading design documents. They will also have a range of language related to the design, and they will go back and forth between text and diagram to better understand the idea she is trying to convey. When Antoinette is communicating with a knowledgeable client or with colleagues, she uses shorthand symbols, straightedge lines with measurements, and other markings that are known to professionals in her field. This type of writing would be inappropriate to others without this base of knowledge. They would see it as a secret code. Before she begins to share any written information, she must consider who the target audience is and how they will best understand what she is attempting to communicate. Without this consideration the entire message could be lost because there would exist a mismatch between the audience and the message.

At another site, Marian Mejia works for an advertising firm that communicates by an internal texting system used by all members of her work community. She also communicates with clients by email. Both colleagues and clients are her audiences and when writing she must first decide what style and language will be most appropriate to ensure clear communication. While her communication with colleagues is friendly and involves texting, her communication with clients is much more formal. With coworkers, advertising lingo, like *creatives*, is often used and messages might be short phrases. With clients, however, emails are longer, more formal in tone, and often invite feedback or are intended to build an understanding of a project's development.

Depending on which group she is addressing, a client or a colleague, Marian has to code-switch from friendly to formal language throughout the day. It's become easier now, but at the start of her employment, she found it challenging. Marian was never taught how to write an email for a client in her college courses. She didn't know what kind of language or sentence length might be appropriate. Her schoolmates were always casual in their communication and mostly she talked to teachers after class. How did Marian learn how to communicate with clients and to differentiate that from her communication with coworkers? At first, she made some mistakes that were quickly and sternly corrected by her supervisors, but soon she learned to pay attention to how others at her company were connecting with clients. She realized that their audiences were their clients. She learned this by looking over the shoulders of her colleagues, with permission, of course, to see how they composed an email. She noticed the tone and language used by department directors. In essence, she sought out models to use as personal scaffolds for her own writing. The models provided insights about strategic writing for a specific audience and about ways to explain information, ideas for communicating questions, and words to use for offering assistance. From Marian's perspective, she had broken the code; she learned how to be a part of the workplace writing community she had joined. She learned to use the language and style needed to communicate with two audiences, her colleagues and clients.

Given the various ways in which written communication occurs in different careers and professions, it behooves us to help our students learn how they can use models to support their communications with each new audience, and how important it is to search for models to help them understand the components of an effective communication style for a particular audience. Whether they choose to become an electrician, who may need to create a schematic with symbols for light bulbs, wires, and resistors, or a dietician who writes blogs, the use of models can help students to build understanding and expertise when it comes to developing their new writing skills. (Light, 2001). Teaching students to search out a model that can serve merely as a guide is sound instructional practice because, "if students are to be successful in school, at work, and in their personal lives, they must learn to write. A basic goal of schooling then is to teach students to use this versatile tool effectively and flexibly" (Graham, 2019). This requires that they receive adequate practice and instruction in writing, as this complex skill does not develop naturally.

PAUSE AND CONSIDER

What are the most common audiences your students write for, both now and in the future? What must they know to enter the "conversation" of these groups? Why is it crucial they do so? Return to these notes and add any new insights about audiences as you read through the scenarios in each chapter.

Further support for the need to teach writing well was noted by The National Council of Teachers of English (NCTE, 2022) in a recent position statement:

> Young people encounter many types of media texts and use many different literacy practices throughout a given day. Everyone in our society now needs the ability to assess the widely varying quality of the information, entertainment, and persuasion that surrounds them, to evaluate the veracity and validity of claims, and to debunk misinformation when necessary. The broadening of the communication landscape opens greater opportunities for

student voice and agency as they move from users and consumers to participators and creators.

Agency lies in being able to write for a variety of situations, to a range of audiences, using the most suitable style and tone for a particular aim. While the debate around the need to write essays in English Language Arts classes is ongoing, many educators agree with the call for "greater relevance and engagement in the classroom" (Schmoker, 2022). If literacy instruction is shared by all content teachers, writing can sit more naturally within the realms that best fit. Science teachers can teach writing of informational science content within the context that it occurs in society—blogs, reports, journal articles, and so forth. Social studies teachers can teach writing through speeches, infographics, and position statements. Math teachers can guide students to compose reports and articles with scaled diagrams, statistical analyses, and data. This builds relevancy and supports a literate cadre of citizens who can lead, manage, and express ideas all through various forms of writing. We advocate for increased writing in a variety of classes in a strategic manner that takes into account the audience receiving the message. It is through writing to a specified target audience that we negotiate meaning, convey ideas, and connect with others.

HOW DO WE SUPPORT STUDENTS IN THINKING ABOUT AUDIENCE WHEN THEY WRITE?

Across all disciplines there are specific questions that student writers need to consider about their audience. Figure 2.3 provides more detailed questions that students can use to think about aspects of the audience that will influence the writing style, language choice, format, tone, and other aspects.

Figure 2.3 • Questions to Consider About the Audience

| Task: |||
| Write _______ for this audience: _____________________________ |||
Questions to Consider About Audience When Writing	**Possibilities**	**Notes to Self in Response to Questions**
Who is my audience?	Are you familiar with the readers of your writing? Are you writing to one individual or to a large group? Are they experts or novices or both? Consider clients you are not familiar with, clients you are familiar with, a boss or superior employee, acquaintances, close friends or colleagues, people who work for you, people you are consulting with, those who are consulting you.	

Questions to Consider about Audience When Writing	Possibilities	Notes to Self in Response to Questions
What background knowledge is needed?	Determine if the audience has extensive background knowledge on the topic, some background knowledge or knows very little. Note which idea best fits with the information being conveyed: Extensive background knowledge is needed to understand the topic; some background knowledge is needed; little or no background knowledge is needed.	
Do they have experience reading about the topic?	Determine if the audience is well read on the topic, has read some, or has not read at all.	
Do they have experience discussing the topic?	Determine if the audience has discussed the topic extensively (with or without you), has discussed some of the topic, or has not discussed the topic.	
What are the points that will be new to them?	Consider background knowledge, experience, and reading when identifying points to be discussed.	
What points do I need examples for?	Anticipate situations that will require an example or exemplar and include it in the text.	
Will they want research documentation?	Determine whether research or data will support understanding or clarification of the topic.	
Will they want to be directed to additional resources?	Identify additional resources for situations that may require augmentation or clarification.	
What style of language will work best for them?	Determine style, which might include Standard English, complete sentences, a mix of standard and colloquial language, incomplete sentences, slang, coded language, formal vocabulary terms, informal vocabulary terms, or ellipses (the omission of one or more words that are obviously understood). Will they understand the terms or symbols being used? Are data tables, charts, graphs, glossaries or other graphics/supports needed?	

THEIR TURN: CONSIDERING AUDIENCE

Using the information shown as Figure 2.3, ask students to choose a target audience they might write to. For example, they might select readers of a gardening blog, visitors to an art gallery reading signage, 4th graders learning about metamorphosis from a library book, senior citizens learning how to make a chart using a document application like Word or Google Docs, a marketing team ready to review a proposal for a new cell phone product, or some other audience with whom they want to communicate. Have them answer the questions in Figure 2.3 using the template found on the online companion, resources.corwin.com/ClassroomToCareer.

Modeling Decisions About Audience

Using models is essential to learning to write in any genre. Many beginning songwriters have modeled their first songs after their studied heroes, before they found their own style and method. Guiding students to seek out and use models is a part of promoting a life skill that will support their success as professionals, trade workers, business owners, citizens with a voice on issues, and in any other area of life where writing comes into play. Like songwriters, in learning to teach most of us have emulated the powerful teachers we've had. We often manage our classrooms, interact with our students, and design instruction with the models of these teachers in mind. Often we have unconsciously studied the teaching behaviors of those we emulate. They are our heroes and their instructional moves have become our practices.

Consider this classroom scenario: Once while teaching a lesson about atoms and molecules, 7th grade teacher Jack Boone asked his students to draw a water molecule. They stared at him, not sure how to proceed. He encouraged them to give it a try. As many attempted the task, one student, Tony, who typically knew exactly how to proceed and succeed, laid his head on the desk and gave up. He said, "I can't picture this and I can't do it." Even with additional encouragement from his table peers he would not try. As the lesson unfolded, Mr. Boone shared a manipulative model of atoms and molecules and the students were able to conclude that they had two oxygen atoms and one hydrogen atom and together they created the water molecule of H_2O. With this visual base, they now had the model they needed to expand their knowledge and to continue their investigations. Mr. Boone had students return to this model throughout the lesson to guide their understanding of how salt dissolves in a water solution.

His ultimate goal was to have students understand how the structure of a water molecule causes it to act as a solvent to a solute like salt. Students needed a model to see how chemical bonds hold hydrogen and oxygen atoms together. As students engaged in lab work to look at salt solubility in water, they returned to their water molecule model to add information about polarity and charge.

How could Mr. Boone expect Tony and his fellow students to create a water molecule sketch if they had never seen one? Likewise, how can we expect students to create various types of writing if they haven't seen a target model or exemplar? It's easy to resolve this issue by showing models when tasking students with writing; however, an even bigger and better goal is to teach them how to seek out their own models. Once out of the K–12 system, young people will encounter writing tasks that will be unfamiliar. Success will depend on their ability to seek out and analyze models as they create their own blogs, discussion posts, letters, articles, proposals, diagrams, commercial scripts and other writing beyond our imagination.

Just like Jack Boone we need to present our students with models that contain different styles, tones, and language. As they examine these, we need to help them realize that the element that defines each model is the audience for whom the intended message is meant. Before writers can craft a particular message or text, they need to have seen an example or at least know where to go to put together a model for themselves. Just like Mr. Boone we need to start off a communication task by sharing a model, and then we need to integrate experiences in the lesson that cause students to return to the model as they design and refine their own communication.

Once students have identified their audience, it's time to share some models of texts written to similar audiences. A strategic use of models can help students to identify a framework from which they can build their own writing. And models will help students see there's no one-size-fits-all approach to writing by helping them to see a variety of approaches.

In order to move the idea that models matter from the classroom into the world of work we need to show this to our students. Yes, we need to model the power of a model by helping them realize that how the text is written, and to whom the text (audience) is being shared involves more than just enjoying the message. To analyze the craft that was used to compose the message, students have to analyze the moves made by the crafter/writer. Here again they must move beyond enjoying the language and the style to considering why the writer chose each.

Students need to practice how to craft a message that is unique to a particular audience. Our goal is to ensure that students begin to think like the writer and by doing so they develop a schema to use as they consider their audience and how they will address them when crafting their own workplace texts. But they must begin to consider the hows of writing the text for the audience.

When writers are tasked with writing to a particular audience by a leader, colleague, or manager, they are given a purpose. In some instances, the writer identifies the purpose, as discussed in chapter 1. Once the purpose is identified, the writer can move on to considering who will read the writing. As we've noted, it's essential to consider many aspects of the audience including experience, background knowledge, and language use. We've also discussed the strategic use of models to identify key aspects of text that fit the audience and the purpose. Outside the classroom setting, students will often have to seek out and analyze their own models. They may have to synthesize aspects of multiple model texts to create their own prototype to fit a circumstance that calls for writing. How can teachers help facilitate this independence? As in most situations where you want students to develop a protocol, allow them time to practice and provide scaffolds. More specifically, offer opportunities for students to practice selecting and using model texts.

Figure 2.4 shares sentence frames that students can use to notice aspects of a model text. Students are guided to pay attention to titles (headings), information at the sentence level, author's purpose, tone, structure, and language. They even consider clarity and organization. These sentence frames can be used to facilitate partner talk about a model text and guide students to consider aspects of a model text they might include in their writing. If they encounter a lack of clarity or cite confusing aspects of a model text, they might also work through ways to improve when they compose their own text.

Figure 2.4 ◆ Sentence Frames to Support the Use of Models

The title (heading) makes me think _______________________________________.

When I look at this sentence, I notice _______________________________________.

Based on my understanding of the author's purpose, _______________________.

The tone suggests ____.

I'm not sure what this word (or sentence) means, however, I will ______________.

The text structure shows _______________________________________.

The language used by the author indicates _______________________________.

The text is organized to highlight _______________________________.

I also notice ____.

THEIR TURN: SUMMARIZE MODEL TEXTS

Here's a way you can guide students to build their own capacity to seek out and use models that fit the purpose and the audience that will read the writing.

First, task students with a purpose that fits within the discipline they are studying. Here are a few examples of reasons to write: write a blog critiquing a newly released song or album or a piece of art, create a proposal for designing an auditorium for an acoustic performance, write a letter to a congress person about an issue—sewage dumped in the local river or ocean, tap water quality concerns, watering of local green spaces, access or lack of access to public spaces like parks, pools, or libraries.

Next, have students seek out two to three model texts that were written for a similar purpose and to a similar audience. Using the sentence frames to document thinking (refer to Figure 2.4), students should analyze the model texts.

Finally, ask students to summarize what they have learned from analyzing their model texts. These are aspects of the models that they will incorporate into their own writing. The template below can facilitate this activity (find a downloadable version online at resources.corwin.com/ClassroomToCareer).

Summarize Model Texts Template

Purpose	(Examples: write a blog critiquing a newly released song or album or a piece of art; create a proposal for designing an auditorium for an acoustic performance; write a letter to a congressman about an issue such as sewage dumped in the local river, ocean, etc., tap water quality, watering of local green spaces, or access to public spaces like parks, pools, or libraries.)		
Find Model Texts	Seek out two to three model texts that were written for a similar purpose and to a similar audience. Using the sentence frames to document thinking, students should analyze the model texts.		
Description of Model Text	**Model text 1 is** ____________.	**Model text 2 is** ____________.	**Model text 3 is** ____________.
Analysis of Model Texts	The title (heading) makes me think ____________. When I look at this sentence, I notice ____________. Based on my understanding of the author's purpose, ____________.	The title (heading) makes me think ____________. When I look at this sentence, I notice ____________. Based on my understanding of the author's purpose, ____________.	The title (heading) makes me think ____________. When I look at this sentence, I notice ____________. Based on my understanding of the author's purpose, ____________.

(Continued)

(Continued)

	The tone suggests ______.	The tone suggests ______.	The tone suggests ______.
	I'm not sure what this word (or sentence) means, however, I will ______.	I'm not sure what this word (or sentence) means, however, I will ______.	I'm not sure what this word (or sentence) means, however, I will ______.
	The text structure shows ______.	The text structure shows ______.	The text structure shows ______.
	The language used by the author indicates ______.	The language used by the author indicates ______.	The language used by the author indicates ______.
	The text is organized to highlight ______.	The text is organized to highlight ______.	The text is organized to highlight ______.
	I also notice ______.	I also notice ______.	I also notice ______.
Summarize: What will I be sure to include in my writing?			

online resources

Composing for a Specific Audience

After writers view models and determine what they want to include in their own writing, they can begin to compose. It's important to note that the use of models to gain insights does not mean that the writing needs to always be identical in format, style, or language. The degree to which a model is mirrored depends on the nature of the writing. If the writer is composing a blog or some other form of writing that is intended to showcase the author's personality, pizazz, or unique style, then the models might be used to see various means of communicating with the aim of thinking outside the box. If, however, the writing is for a situation that requires communication in a more strictly conforming way, the models serve as guides to the required mode of writing.

For example in Carol Williams's 10th grade science class students look at model texts used in various STEAM-related careers, including some of the ones mentioned earlier in this chapter—architect, electrician, science blogger, lab scientist, science teacher, and science newspaper columnist. Miss Williams's lesson includes the following points:

- Sharing learning intentions

- Presenting a think-aloud

- Inviting partner talk

- Promoting student practice

- Engaging students in self-assessment or peer feedback

Miss Williams has gathered examples to share. To introduce students to the nuances of composing for specific audiences, she uses a think-aloud strategy to help them understand what to notice when looking at an architect's text. Think-aloud might be an instructional strategy you choose to use often because it allows your students to see how an expert (you) thinks through a task or a passage. Before beginning the think-aloud, **Ms. Williams shares the learning intentions with students,** which clearly describe what she wants them to know, understand, and be able to do as a result of instruction.

Notice the text Miss Williams uses is an actual architect's plan.

Here's a little except from Miss Williams's **think-aloud:**

> I'm going to share our learning intentions for today which are to understand how architects use a plan to convey what they intend to build. Additionally, you will become familiar with and be able to use architectural language. You will get to use this language in some of the activities in this lesson.

Once Ms. Williams finished sharing the content, language, and social intentions, she continued thinking aloud about the content:

> Well, this is an interesting drawing. It's very precise and technical. I think this is written for people who have an understanding of measurements, angles, and related terminology. The author was writing to an audience who they believed had a strong knowledge and language base regarding structural elements. I also see that there is text listed that adds to the diagram and describes elements, like the driveway and sidewalk. I also see words that are unfamiliar to me—"grading and seeding"—and think seeding relates to plants. I think they are going to create some landscaping. I know this is a design for a house—I see that labeled in the middle of the picture. It's one story with a two-car garage. I also see there is a legend. I remember that from graphing—we have a key or legend that will help me to identify some of the elements in the illustration. It seems that the audience for this graphic are the builders who will be creating this structure. I wonder who will explain it to the homeowners?

Scan the QR code to view the architect's drawing discussed in Miss Williams's think-aloud. You can find it in Figure 8.2 (p. 77) of the QR code link.

URL: https://www.slideshare.net/AdityaSanyal3/architectural-working-drawings-146157041

Notice that Ms. Williams focused on the audience for the plan and pointed out that the language and structure were technical. The plan was intended for a person other than a novice. She continued her think-aloud, noting elements of the text that she believed would be understood by an audience with sophisticated knowledge and also considered questions in case the plan might be more difficult to understood by the homeowner who possibly had less technical skill and language. Remember, her goal was to show students how to notice elements in a writing sample from a workplace scenario and to identify who the audience for the text might be.

Before sending students on their way to craft a message to an identified audience, Miss Williams thinks aloud about what a homeowner might want to know about an architect's drawing. To do this, she goes back to the drawing and revisits her initial noticings of the diagram. Here's an *excerpt from Miss William's think-aloud* to support students' writing to the homeowner:

> I'm going to go back to the architect's drawing before I begin to craft my letter to the homeowners. I want to think about what the homeowners will want to know and learn. I think I will start with a friendly greeting and explain who I am. Then I'll reference the drawing and will tell them about the house. I'll note that it's a one-story home with a spacious two-car garage. They also might want to know about the exterior of the house, so I'll start with the driveway, which extends to the sidewalk. Then I'll describe the backyard and will mention the adjacent wooded area. They might be interested in knowing there are beautiful trees near their backyard. I see that there are words like gas main and water main on the diagram, so maybe I should mention that these are being installed. They will want to know that lines for utilities are being put in place. I intend to end by mentioning a nice feature of the house, so I'll share about the porch. I'll paint a mental picture for the homeowners, so they can imagine themselves in this house. They would enjoy relaxing on the porch in the evening. Finally, I'll conclude by letting the homeowners know that I can answer any questions they might have—they can email me. I'll sign it and add my phone number. That's it. Now I can get started writing.

Once Miss Williams feels she has showcased enough of the elements that she wants students to practice—going back and forth between text and drawing, noticing vocabulary, and noting dimension and measurements— she asks students to engage in **partner talk**, which is another effective instructional collaborative strategy that involves students working in pairs to discuss and share their thoughts and ideas about the material being presented. During partner talk, Miss Wiliams encourages students to use their academic school vocabulary to talk about a similar diagram, with text, and to try to identify the intended audience by noticing the author's language and structure. She also shares a resource—an architecture glossary—to support their language learning.

Scan this QR code for the architecture glossary. http://bit .ly/3ZWGKpl

THEIR TURN: PARTNER TALK

Using Miss Williams's think-aloud as a guide, engage students in partner talk about the architect's drawing. Invite students to practice crafting an explanation of the architect's plan for a different audience—the homeowners. Explain that the homeowners are novices in terms of architecture knowledge, but they still have a vested interest in the design of this house. The homeowners want detailed information, however, they don't have the same background knowledge as the expert architects. Have students give it a try. How might they craft this message to the homeowners?

Purpose: Working with a partner, write a paragraph that explains the major design features shown in the architect's drawing to the homeowners that have hired this architecture firm. Given an understanding of this audience, you can include illustrations, diagrams, definitions or any other clarifying elements that would meet their needs.
Audience: homeowners
Writing:

Self-assessment check: I have . . .

- Addressed my audience with a professional greeting.

- Included body of information that expresses the intent.

- Within the body, defined words the audience may not know, for example: cantilever, roof overhang, and easement.

- Closed with contact information.

- Included my signature.

(Continued)

(Continued)

To guide students through the process of composing while attending to audience, provide a checklist that could eventually be used as a mental schema for writing in any situation. Figure 2.5 offers a checklist protocol that students can use in school and then incorporate into their own metacognitive schema for use outside of school settings when they are tasked with writing. Have students use the checklist to move through the process of writing within the context of a content area—science, math, English, social studies, music, and so forth. You can assign the purpose and audience or let students choose, if appropriate. Additionally, you can incorporate the previous tools for using model texts and for peer review. (This checklist can be downloaded from the companion website, resources.corwin.com/ClassroomToCareer.)

Figure 2.5 • Checklist for Writing

Writing Steps	Did I Do This? (✓)	Notes
Identify the purpose		
Identify the audience and their needs as readers of my writing.		
Seek out model text(s) to review; identify elements to include in my own text for the target audience.		
Compose my text for my target audience.		
Share my text with a peer to get feedback related to addressing the audience.		
Revise based on feedback and my own review.		

Peer Feedback to Focus on Audience

While models are useful for beginning the process of writing to address a given audience, peer feedback can be useful for fine-tuning the draft with a focus on the audience. Feedback benefits both the recipient and the giver of the feedback. When you review a peer's work, you also think about your own writing, especially in terms of clarity and revision. To reap the benefits of feedback focused on audience, have each student work with a partner to share their writing. Peers can use the *Writing for an Audience Peer Feedback* form (downloadable from the online companion), which asks peers to respond and make suggestions based on the following prompts:

- Is the text written for the target audience? Provide insights and details in your response.

- Will the audience be able to understand the text clearly? Explain your response and note language, charts, definitions, text complexity, and so forth.

- Is there anything else you'd like to share with your partner about their writing?

Because self-assessment is as essential to writing as peer review, students should be guided to take a final look at their writing before sending it off to the reader(s). Figure 2.6 shows a self-assessment rubric that students may use to evaluate their own efforts at composing a text for an audience. The rubric serves as a reminder of what to include when using a model to write and focuses them on what to think about when addressing a target audience to communicate a message, sentiment, or idea(s). (Download the rubric from the online companion, too: resources.corwin .com/ClassroomToCareer.)

Figure 2.6 • Student Self-Assessment Rubric Focused on Audience

Student Name: ____

CATEGORY	3	2	1
Key elements of a model text are used in my writing to address the target audience. *****	My writing addresses the audience using many aspects of the model text(s)—format, style, language, etc.	My writing addresses the audience using a few aspects of the model text(s)—format, style, language, etc.	My writing addresses the audience using only one aspect of the model text(s)—format, style, language, etc.
My writing communicates my message, sentiment, or idea(s) clearly to my audience.	My writing offers language, visuals, and information that clarify my intent.	My writing offers language, visuals, and information that partially clarify my intent.	My writing offers language, visuals, and information minimally clarify my intent.

*****This criteria can be used when the writing is intended to mirror the model text(s).

SUM IT UP

While much has been learned about how writing is taught (A. Applebee & Langer, 2011), little is known about how writing is useful in workplace situations. We, like Gallagher (2011) and Graham (2019), believe that students must be taught that the audiences for their writing are larger than their peers and teachers and also that they will be called upon to write for new audiences in any profession they choose to enter. It's therefore essential that as budding writers, they learn to consider the audience when crafting a document, blog, text, email, or other form of written communication or information. Knowing the interests, backgrounds, expertise, and intentions of the audience guides the writer in the development of a meaningful, authentic piece of writing that will be clear, focused, and informative for the intended readers. Using models is something that many of us who have been in the workplace for a while know how to do, but it's likely taken years of practice to gain proficiency doing so. And we've probably stumbled along the way, sending off texts with glaring mistakes in style, tone, or language that leave email recipients, project clients, or even faculty colleagues bewildered. The goal of teaching students to address an audience is to guide them to maneuver through the ever-changing world of written communication in a navigable manner. A strategic use of models can help students to identify a framework from which they can build their own writing. Students need to learn the value of reviewing a model, learning from it, and then applying ideas gleaned. When teachers show students how to do this, the use of models for writing becomes a lifelong skill that will serve them well in their futures as they address a wide array of audiences.

ANTICIPATION GUIDE

Revisit the anticipation guide that appeared at the beginning of the chapter to check and expand your initial responses. Even if you had the correct answer, now you can add an explanation that illustrates your deepened understanding.

Possible Fact	True	False	What else can you add?
When writing a message, regardless of the audience, the same tone, style, and structure must be used.		X Some audiences require less formal language structures and tone.	
Code-switching is appropriate depending on the audience.	X		
Most professions require writing, except for professions involving math.		X Mathematicians are often required to write scaled diagrams, statistical analyses, and share data.	

CHAPTER THREE

Language
What's the Best Way to Say It?

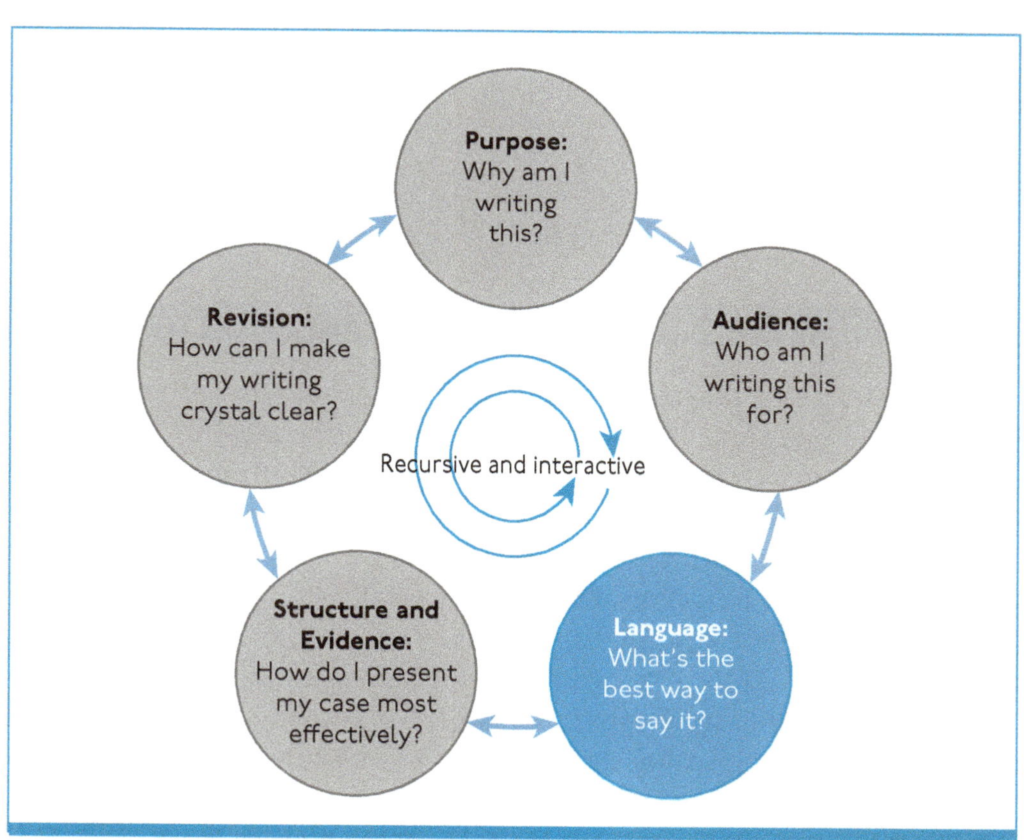

We cannot control the way people interpret our ideas or thoughts, but we can control the words and tones we choose to convey them.

— Suzy Kassem, American writer, poet, philosopher

ANTICIPATION GUIDE

The focus of this chapter is on *language*. Before you begin reading this chapter, check your knowledge of the following information that will be shared throughout. In the *Sum It Up* section at the conclusion of the chapter, you'll be able to revisit these points and self-assess what you've learned. Use this anticipation guide to assess your beginning understanding:

Possible Fact	True	False
The term *language registers* refers to the degree of formality and informality used to communicate in different situations.		
Academic writing centers mostly in standard language, so it is best to teach students using a model in standard English.		
Students benefit more from writing tasks designed within the context of their discipline rather than those that span multiple content areas.		

In which situations do you stop to think about what you are about to say and how to best say it? Probably this attention to your words happens in situations when you are conversing with others with whom you don't share a personal register or a familiar set of understandings and also when you are conveying information that requires great accuracy. It sounds like you are at work or in a professional situation if this is the experience! In less formal situations we just share ideas without concentrating on the words we are choosing. Our words matter and especially in professional situations. It's important for students to learn how to make decisions about language, especially because the language they use with one another may be different than that used in an academic or professional settings—and language choices will vary according to purpose and audience.

WHAT DO WE MEAN WHEN WE TALK ABOUT LANGUAGE?

In some situations, language serves as a gatekeeper, a purveyor of selective access, and a pusher of inequity. Language knowledge permits those who are fluent to enter and restricts access when a person doesn't have the right words, tone, or style. This chapter is not about teaching students to write a certain way. It does not assume that there is a correct professional way to communicate. In fact, we advocate for equity through an understanding that there are multiple registers and many dialects, and we acknowledge that language changes. Brown (2019) explains it this way: "Language often stands as a barrier. Multilingual students [who] flow brilliantly back and forth between Spanish, English, Khmer, and various cultural dialects are simply not afforded the ability to use the intellectual resources that define their home environments."

Instead, the aim of this chapter is to support the facilitation of student writers to learn the language of a work or other culture, so that they can write and be understood within a given context. This knowledge will allow for creativity and innovation when writing. For instance, if the work writing environment is about breaking boundaries, novelty, or invention, a writer should review the standards of practice and the style used by others in this work environment for the purpose of identifying practice, determining how to shift and restyle while understanding what exists. Our goal in this chapter is to help teachers to provide student writers with the knowledge regarding how and what to observe, learn about, and make change as assessed.

YOUR TURN: REFLECTION AND PREPARATION

Think of all the different audiences you write for in a week. Now, think about the language choices you make for each of those communications. How does your use of language shift depending on who you are writing to? For example, how does an email to a parent differ from a text message to your best friend? Consider collecting models you can share with students to illustrate the different ways we adjust our language based on our audience and how widely those audiences vary.

____

____

____

____

____

____

WHY SHOULD WE FOCUS ON UNDERSTANDING LANGUAGE?

The language of a profession is dynamic and situational. While most of today's educators suggest it's important to learn the language of their discipline if one is to have successful communications with others about related topics, 11th grade math teacher Mr. Andy Clement is even more specific regarding his expectations for communication in math. He realizes that *math language* varies, depending on the situation, the audience, and on the work environment. He provides two examples of math language in different contexts: a loan officer presenting information to potential clients and a chief operations officer (COO) presenting information to the bank's board of directors.

First, a loan officer in a bank communicating about interest rates and time frames for repayment might employ language that clarifies or explains options to customers. He might put himself into the shoes of the customer by saying, "You have two options. Let's look at both and you can decide what's better for you." Then he would share a written plan incorporating the information they discussed using charts and payment lists. The loan officer's language is specific and concise. His customers want to know terms, rates, down payments, and eligibility. The written plan he offers provides lists that facilitate easy comparisons between options. The text is bold and there are highlighted areas to indicate standout sections that he wants readers to notice such as special loans for first-time buyers. The document has illustrations and photos to help guide readers to understand specific aspects of the options. For instance, there's a section with illustrations that represent various types of loans, like adjustable-rate, fixed-rate, and conventional loans. The loan officer uses this clear, to-the-point document to accompany his discussion of the various options. Customers can listen while also focusing attention on the key ideas that the loan officer points to on the document. Additionally, the customers can take this document home to review their options while they are deciding.

In another situation, a chief operations officer (COO) might explain how to solve a problem to the board of directors by saying, "We are focusing on recruiting for areas in which we are lacking skills to meet the new demands of our technologically savvy clientele," as she shared a document detailing the "next steps" plans in bulleted form. Here the COO is discussing growth with a marketing focus and a positive intent. She addresses the weakness and steers clients toward the solution, using a handout that scripts the salient points of her talk. This problem-solution literary device she shares is indicative of the language she often uses to show how, under her leadership, the organization is resolving issues. Her verbal announcement is paired with text that provides a shorthand version of her talking points. It's a tactic used to indicate prospective growth and to muster enthusiasm for the tasks ahead. She is successful because she has transferred her knowledge about the importance of detailing information about the audience to create a profile that she can use to share some fairly complex information.

Both the loan officer and the COO have a good chance of successfully sharing information with their targeted audience because they thought carefully about who their audience was, the audience's knowledge of the topic, and the language style-register that would be effective to share information with their key audience.

Both speakers studied and used math to interact, but the language they employed in their writing depended on the audience and the situation. Their interactions were successful because they considered all the dimensions of language shown in Figure 3.1. Their writing engaged their audience with appropriate language, including style and word choice best suited to share the information and communicate effectively.

Figure 3.1 • Choosing the Best Language for Audience Example

Questions to Consider About Audience When Writing	Possibilities: Make Your Choice by Evaluating the Knowledge of Your Audience	Notes for My Writing
Who is my audience?	Clients you are not familiar with, clients you are familiar with, a boss or superior employee, acquaintances, close friends or colleagues, people who work for you, people you are consulting with, those who are consulting you.	*My audience is someone I don't know who I am informing of an issue.*
What background knowledge is needed?	Audience has extensive background knowledge on the topic, audience has some background knowledge, audience knows very little.	*I don't think my audience has extensive background, but maybe has a little background.*
Do they have experience reading about the topic?	Audience is well read on the topic, has read some, or has not read at all.	*Possibly has read some.*
Do they have experience discussing the topic?	Audience has discussed the topic extensively (with or without you), has discussed some of the topic, or has not discussed the topic.	*The audience has never discussed the topic publicly according to my research online.*
What are the points that will be new to them?	Consider background knowledge, experience, and reading when identifying points to be discussed.	*Since I'm discussing the power plant in my neighborhood, I want to inform the elected official that the air quality has*

(Continued)

(Continued)

Questions to Consider About Audience When Writing	Possibilities: Make Your Choice by Evaluating the Knowledge of Your Audience	Notes for My Writing
		declined greatly since the construction of the plant. I'm going to reference this EPA information: https://www.epa.gov/airmarkets/power-plants-and-neighboring-communities *I'm going to share comments from people in the community, collected when I conducted a survey.*
What points do I need examples for?	Anticipate situations that will require an example or exemplar and include in the text.	*I will need to be very specific since I'm writing about the power plant in my neighborhood. I might share this related example about another town: https://www.npr.org/2022/05/27/1101837180/a-minnesota-town-wants-to-replace-its-coal-plant-with-solar-some-locals-arent-ha*
Will they want research documentation?	Determine whether research or data will support understanding or clarification of the topic.	*I will share power plant emissions data: https://www.epa.gov/newsreleases/epa-issues-power-plant-emissions-data-2021*
Will they want to be directed to additional resources?	Identify additional resources for situations that may require augmentation or clarification.	*I'll add links to the references that I will offer as evidence and examples.*
What style of language will work best for them?	Standard English, complete sentences, a mix of standard and colloquial language, incomplete sentences, slang, coded language, formal vocabulary terms, informal vocabulary terms, ellipses (the omission of one or more words that are obviously understood).	*I will use standard English and will write in a formal style.*

YOUR TURN: PLANNING FOR PURPOSEFUL WRITING

Try using the *Choosing the Best Language for Audience* chart to select the best words to communicate a written message. Imagine that you are writing to your principal to propose a new course to be offered in your department (math, English, science, history/social studies, music, etc.). Knowing that the principal and other members of the administration will be the recipients and readers of your course proposal and an accompanying letter, work through the questions in Figure 3.1 to plan your language register. (You can download a printable version of this chart, with a column for notes, from the online companion, resources.corwin.com/ClassroomToCareer.)

THEIR TURN: PLANNING FOR PURPOSEFUL WRITING

Choose a topic that is relevant to your content area and ask students to use the chart *Choosing the Best Language for Audience* (example in Figure 3.1; template downloadable from online companion) to complete the following task.

Provide these instructions to students:

You want to write a letter to an elected official, for instance, a member of Congress, regarding __________ (education issues, equity in healthcare, environmental issues, safety in your community, science, space, technology, veteran's issues, etc.). You think that the elected official is somewhat familiar with the topic, but you want to provide more insights and details on a personal level and from a local perspective.

Figure 3.1 shows an example of student responses in italics. The responses were written by a student in a science class who planned to write to an elected official about a neighborhood power plant. You might want to use the example in italics in the chart below to model for students how to make the best use of the chart.

Language Registers

The term *language registers* refers to the degree of formality and informality used to communicate in different situations. Language registers are often labeled in these categories: formal, casual, intimate, private, frozen, and consultative (Morrison, 2017) (see Figure 3.2).

- *Formal* language is typically impersonal and used in formal settings (*i.e.*, churches, courts, formal public events like an inauguration).
- *Casual* register is used by social acquaintances or friends and can feature slang, vulgarity, and colloquialisms.
- *Intimate* register is used between close family, intimate partners, and reflects private communications that are not shared with anyone else.
- *Private* refers to self-talk or language we use when we are practicing self-reflection.
- *Frozen* register is unchanging or fixed; frozen language is typically memorized and repeated in specific situations, like the pledge of allegiance or a national anthem.
- *Consultative* register occurs in professional settings, like a doctor's office or during consultations between people seeking and offering professional advice.

Figure 3.2 • How Should I Say It? Example

Language Register	What It Means	What It Looks Like—Example	What I Need to Use for My Writing and Why
formal	For general information that is carefully thought out and typically communicated to strangers or people the author is not closely familiar with. Also used in socially formal situations. Use of standard language and complete sentences.	We are brought together for this momentous occasion upon which degrees will be conferred upon those who have worked diligently for four years.	*I think I may need elements of formal language because I am reaching out to a university, which is a professional setting.*
casual (informal)	Informal, used for acquaintances, colleagues, and peers; a mix of standard and nonstandard language; some slang or colloquial language may be used	Based on the report, I think we should go ahead with the design project. What do you think?	**Since I am offering services and advice, maybe I should try a more consultative tone (friendly and approachable).**
intimate	Very close acquaintances and family members; communication for personal thoughts, may include incomplete sentences, coded words, ellipsis, colloquial language and slang.	Hey! How's it going? We are going to dinner before the show. Coming?	
private	Intra-personal, self-talk, journaling, innermost thoughts, may include standard and nonstandard language, slang, coded words, etc.	I'm thinking about my next moves—should I go to college or should I get a job first? My mom says college, but whoa, I'm not sure.	
frozen	For formal and informal situations; creed-like, legal documents, standard and some non-standard language	We pledge to do what is righteous and just for those who struggle in this world because of discrimination.	
consultative	Formal or informal language that includes feedback to the speaker from the listener; advice or information often provided; both standard and nonstandard language	Have you considered the options of accepting this positive versus the other position? You'll need to think about the benefits package as well as the salary.	

online resources

In Juana Moreno's 9th grade classroom, students identify the register of writing that is most appropriate for their text; for example, they ask themselves, should it be formal, intimate, private, and so forth? Once the register is identified by considering the familiarity that will exist between the speaker and the audience, they select the corresponding language needed to communicate appropriately for their audience. Ms. Moreno has students first use the *Questions to Consider Chart* to identify the type of writing they are doing (refer to Figures 3.1). This focuses students on these elements: language, background knowledge that exists or is needed, experience or lack of experience of the reader, points to be made, examples, research data, additional resources, and language that is most suitable. Then Ms. Moreno has students think about language register by using the *How Should You Say It?* chart (see Figure 3.2 for an example; you can download a printable version from resources.corwin.com/ClassroomToCareer).

Student Brenden is planning to write an email to a potential client of a software company in his attempt to sell a program used to secure and house training videos. He's using the *How Should I Say It?* to think about the examples and details he might add to his email. The chart helps Brenden to determine that his writing should be mostly casual with a few elements of formality, including the use of complete sentences throughout (refer to figure 3.2). He's not writing with the formality of the Declaration of Independence, nor is he writing a text message to his best friend; he's instead bridging the gap between formal and informal.

Ms. Moreno has made it clear to students that sometimes you may choose to use elements of more than one register. What truly matters is that you assess the audience, the goals, and the situation to best determine the language register. That's exactly what Brenden has done in his writing (see Figure 3.3). Notice that Brenden uses complete sentences, but also adds easy-to-read bullet points to highlight the features of his software. His language register is just on the edge of formal—this is intentional because Brenden decided it was important to be friendly and approachable since he's trying to get future clients to feel comfortable contacting him.

Figure 3.3 • Brenden's Email to a Potential Client

February 23, xxxx

Hello to the Department of Education at Birmington State University,

I represent Lightning Rod Software Development. I'm writing to let you know about the latest innovations in storing and housing video for training your students and colleagues. Our software creates a classroom-like environment and our new features are probably beyond any you have seen yet. Our software allows for all of this:

- Annotating video with comments

- Splicing up video into manageable segments

- Easy uploads with built-in compression

- Use on any PC

I'm happy to set up a video conference demonstration of all our features. Please let me know your availability, and we can meet online so I can share our great developments. I look forward to hearing from you soon.

Sincerely yours,
Brenden Marston
bmarston@lighning.com
619-223-xxxx

THEIR TURN: STUDENTS PRACTICE PREWRITING

Ask students to choose a person working in a field related to your content area. Some discipline-specific examples include:

- math – a statistician who is going to analyze data and create graphs to show emergency response teams about their response times to incidents;

- science – a lab scientist doing matching for donor blood transfusions;

- social studies – an historian working at a state history museum that preserves and displays archived documents;

- ELA - the head librarian of a public library who will be organizing an author book reading series for the public;

- music – a choral director of a community choir getting ready to present choices for this years' spring musical;

- art - a home stager or interior designer compiling tile samples for a kitchen and bathroom renovation in an historic home.

Task students with this: *Imagine you are preparing to compose an email in which you are requesting to do a virtual interview with a person who works in the field of _____. Use the How Should I Say It? chart to determine what kind of language you will use to communicate with that person.*

Example responses are noted in italics in the chart in Figure 3.4. You could use this to model how to use the chart, which is what students should be focused on in this prewriting stage. Make it clear that when writing letters they can gather ideas from the examples shown in the *How Should I Say It?* chart. (Download a template version of the chart online at resources.corwin.com/ClassroomToCareer.)

Figure 3.4 • How Should I Say It? Example – Librarian

Language Register	What It Means	What It Looks Like	What I Need to Use for My Writing and Why
formal	For general information that is carefully thought out and typically communicated to strangers or people the author is not closely familiar with. Also used in socially formal situations. Use of standard language and complete sentences.	We are brought together for this momentous occasion upon which degrees will be conferred upon those who have work diligently for four years.	*Because I am writing to the head librarian of the public library, I'm going to use mostly formal language, but since I want to be friendly,*

Language Register	What It Means	What It Looks Like	What I Need to Use for My Writing and Why
casual (informal)	Informal, used for acquaintances, colleagues, and peers; a mix of standard and nonstandard language; some slang or colloquial language may be used.	Based on the report, I think we should go ahead with the design project. What do you think?	*I will add some casual phrases.*
intimate	Very close acquaintances and family members; communication for personal thoughts, may include incomplete sentences, coded words, ellipses, colloquial language and slang.	Hey! How's it going? We are going to dinner before the show. Coming?	*I might say, "Hello Ms. Jones, I am writing to request a video conference with you so that I can learn about your job*
private	Intra-personal, self-talk, journaling, innermost thoughts, may include standard and non-standard language, slang, coded words, etc.	I'm considering my next moves—should I go to college or should I get a job first? My mom says college, but whoa, I'm not sure.	*and how it's changed over the course of your career (formal start). I have always loved books*
frozen	For formal and informal situations; creed-like, legal documents, standard and some nonstandard language	We pledge to do what is righteous and just for those who struggle in this world because of discrimination.	*and want to meet with someone else that does, too (a bit more*
consultative	Formal or informal language that includes feedback to the speaker from the listener; advice or information often provided; both standard and nonstandard language	Have you considered the options of accepting this positive versus the other position? You'll need to think about the benefits package as well as the salary.	*casual).*

Note: This example was created by a student for their target audience, a librarian who is being asked for an interview about her workplace experiences and duties. Like Brenden, this student has been careful to consider the language register that will be most appropriate for her audience.

Language Varieties

We've talked about the importance of considering language registers, but there's another aspect of language to think about when writing—*language varieties*. It doesn't take long to realize that language is not stagnant. There are new words that go from the street corners to the dictionary in virtually no time flat, all the time. Language is dynamic, changing, and growing. Given this, it's important for writers to know about the subgroups, or varieties of language that can be used for writing. We'll consider these: standard, jargon, colloquial, slang, and dialect:

- *Standard* is the form of language that follows the grammar rules and usual structures.

- *Jargon* is more specialized and may include vocabulary that is connected to a particular discipline like medicine or law. Terms like *due diligence* in business or *dek* in journalism are examples of jargon.

- *Colloquial* is language used in ordinary, casual conversations and includes terms like *buzz off, feeling blue,* and *gonna.*

- *Slang*, to contrast, is very informal and is restricted to a particular context or group of people. Words like *hater* or *kick the bucket* are examples of slang. There is sometimes an overlap between colloquial and slang terms.

- *Dialect* is a type of language specific to a group of people or community. In some communities, for example, the term *britches* is used instead of *pants* and *mess of* is used to describe a large quantity.

While our focus in this chapter has been on practical writing, you might find in the workplace, staples of the ELA classroom such as literary devices still prove useful in determining which approach to language is the best to use.

PAUSE AND CONSIDER

What types of language varieties do your students regularly use? Which ones do they need more help with? How can you capitalize on the language expertise they already bring to your classroom? Return and add more as you explore our different examples of teaching language in various scenarios.

It's important to consider audience and background knowledge when deciding if standard language with some jargon sprinkled throughout is appropriate or if adding a bit of colloquial or dialect would be acceptable at all. We suggest guiding students to identify their target language variety using the *Language Variety Planning Chart* (Figure 3.5). From his previous analysis of his planned writing, Brenden knew that he needed a mix of informal and formal. He decided that standard with some jargon would be best. To add a touch of friendliness—important when garnering new clients—Brenden included some colloquial terms. This rounded out his email to provide the clear, technical elements he wanted to sound like a professional in his field, with the approachable aspects needed to gather a client. (Find a printable version of this chart on the online companion, resources.corwin.com/ClassroomToCareer.)

Figure 3.5 • Language Variety Planning Chart Example

Language Variety	Definition	What Terms Might I Use?
standard	Uses grammatical rules and structures	*Represent, innovations*
jargon	Specialized with vocabulary that comes from a discipline	*Splicing, compression, annotating*
colloquial	Used in ordinary, casual conversations	*We can meet online*
slang	Informal, restricted to a group of people	*None needed*
dialect	Specific to a group	*None needed*

Note: Below is Brenden's completed assessment of language variety in advance of writing.

THEIR TURN: USING LANGUAGE VARIETY

Have students explore language variety by adding more to their emails of request to virtually interview a person who works in the field of _________. Then have students use the *Language Variety Planning Chart* to determine what kind of language they are using or should use to communicate their message (see example in Figure 3.5; downloadable available from online companion).

Model using the example in italics in the example below. Be sure to let students know that not all writing has all language varieties. The example includes two varieties of language.

(Continued)

(Continued)

EXAMPLE OF LANGUAGE VARIETY PLANNING CHART

Language Variety	Definition	What terms might I use?
standard	Uses grammatical rules and structures	• *I am writing to request* • *catalog books* • *A great book is like a ride through the universe. It's a journey. (a metaphor that a book-lover might understand).*
jargon	Specialized with vocabulary that comes from a discipline	
colloquial	Used in ordinary, casual conversations	• *side notes*
slang	Informal, restricted to a group of people	
dialect	Specific to a group	

Here's the text that was composed using the example chart that assessed language variety in advance of writing the email to the librarian:

Hello Ms. Jones,

I am writing to request a video conference with you so that I can learn about your job and how it's changed over the course of your career. I have always loved books and want to meet with someone else that does, too. I am a student at Jackson High School and am looking at careers that I might be interested in before I start applying to college. I mentioned that I enjoy reading. A great book is like a ride through the universe. It's a journey. I'm also a soccer player and play in the school jazz band. Those are just a few side notes about me. Mostly, I would like to know a bit about you and your career as a librarian. I'm wondering how you organize and catalog books. I'd also like to hear how you provide resources for people researching in the library. If you are interested in meeting with me, please let me know when you are available for a video call and I'll set it up. Thank you so much.

—Serena Kingsly

HOW DO WE SUPPORT STUDENTS IN THINKING ABOUT LANGUAGE WHEN THEY WRITE?

We've explored the classroom and tools that students can use to plan for and engage the audience, and considered language registers and language variety. Now let's consider how this extends into future writing experiences that students may actually encounter in work situations.

For illustration's sake, let's consider two English majors whose career paths were different: One, whom we'll call Lily Gonzalez, is a food blogger, and one, whom we'll call Jasmine Ralph, is a journalist for a local online newspaper. Both produce texts that inform and provide references. Both write for a general public audience and both make their living by writing. Lily writes to an audience that consists predominantly of women between the ages of twenty-five and forty. They are young professionals who want to learn about cooking healthy foods for themselves. Her target demographic has specific needs, and the language she uses speaks to them in an intentional manner. Unlike the math language we considered at the start of this chapter, Lily doesn't use language that discusses options or has authoritarian phrases. She needs to relate, like a close friend, to her readers. In one blog, she writes, "You know, sometimes I'm on the freeway, tired after a long day and on the verge of driving through a fast-food restaurant window, when I tell myself, 'Lily, remember that fish and veggie plate you pre-prepared on the weekend? That's what you're having tonight!" Did you notice how she used relatable language to connect with her readership? She even tapped into a *private* language register, to create a journal-like piece.

Jasmine, to contrast, uses the traditional newspaper style to inform the public of the latest happenings. In her last article, Jasmine began her column by writing, "A family of three narrowly escaped a fire that started in the kitchen and engulfed their home. Firefighters responded to a 911 call from the home just after 6 p.m. While the family is shaken, patriarch Sean Black says he is grateful for the quick response that saved the lives of himself, his wife, and three-year-old son." Jasmine's style is concise and to the point. She knows that she has limited space to get the story out and that every word must be important. She shares column space with other writers and knows she must paint a vivid, accurate picture in a pithy, straightforward way.

These are just two examples from a world of language registers and varieties in professional writing. Teachers can model examples from your disciplines to help students make decisions about the best language to use for specific audience and purpose in their writing.

PAUSE AND CONSIDER

How could students learn about the language commonly used in writing genres that are unfamiliar to them?

____

____

____

____

____

Modeling and Dissecting Writing Artifacts

While the research on disciplinary literacy is clear—students need access to writing tasks within the context of a discipline (Wilson-Lopez & Bean, 2017)—teachers often find it challenging to design such writing lessons. Identifying the situation within which the writing will sit is a top priority. One of the best ways to teach writing is through the presentation and analysis of actual writing in authentic situations. We call this dissecting writing artifacts and we'll get to that later in this chapter. Before that, though, students need to see models of the type of writing they are expected to produce.

Consider Moriah Makeda, a young employee working in a growing division of media production. Her business studies at the university prepared her to think in critical, business-sense terms, but they didn't prepare her for corresponding with clients, designing projects on shared documents with colleagues, and developing written reports to be presented at meetings. How did she learn how to do it? In Moriah's own words, "I had to look at the documents that the veteran employees were sending me. I tried to match their patterns, style, and language. Interestingly, I had to learn the language of my co-workers. Terms like *deck of, creative,* or *broad strokes* weren't taught in Econ 121, but I had to know them and use them. Fortunately, I had mentors who taught me to review other writing, to capture the essence of it for myself. And that's just what I did!"

While no teacher can accurately predict where a student will be employed in the future, nor what her future writing tasks will be, all teachers can prepare students to dissect writing artifacts from their current situation. As we've discussed in chapter 2, through modeling and guided instruction, students can learn how to acquire writing samples to review that illustrate the type of writing they will encounter in their future workplaces. They can learn to use tools of inquiry to match the language of their employer, coworkers, or their clients by (1) interviewing professionals in a chosen field, (2) analyzing what their interview subjects share, (3) discussing it with a partner, and (4) dissecting an example of writing provided by the interview subject. The following pages provide examples of how to do this with students.

Interview Professionals.

Language learning, which begins early in a child's life, never ends, and one way to capture the language of a discipline in a specific context is to interview a professional from that area of practice. There are two benefits to this. First, you can hear the language being used. Second, you can document notable elements in writing. Transcription is a helpful way to capture the content for later in-depth analysis.

For example, in Mr. Souza's 9th grade Advisory classroom, students are tasked with interviewing a person in a place of employment that is interesting to them. Mr. Souza has secured a few volunteers from various professions for this assignment but is open to having students interview family members or friends, too. Susana is intrigued with the profession of medicine. She knows that becoming a doctor means lots of studying and years of school. She wants to know what it's like to be a medical student. Mr. Souza has contacted a medical student who has agreed to respond to five interview questions by email. Below is a transcript of that interview. Additionally, the medical student, Chris Brant, has provided the class with a copy of his study notes as an artifact for Mr. Souza's students to dissect (see Figure 3.7 later in this chapter). They do so by setting them up in a question-answer format because this makes it easier for their discussions.

What kind of writing do you do in your profession?

Right now, I'm writing notes that are offered by professors during lecture, and I take notes from my reading assignments [see figure 3.7]. They are detailed. I label and annotate sketches that are important. The doctors I work with in the clinic take notes about patients. I'm learning to do this. Oftentimes the notes are responses by the patient, given after the doctor makes an inquiry. A doctor might ask, How frequently do your migraines occur? Or do you feel pain in your knee only when you are walking? They record these responses as documentation of the patient's condition. The notes are shorthand codes and are entered electronically in most cases nowadays. Diagnoses are also recorded.

When you write to your medical student colleagues or your professors, what are the topics you discuss? Are there special words or terms that you use?

When I write to other med students, it's much more casual. I still use the medical terminology, but I don't pay as much attention to formality. When I write to professors, I draft and then edit my own work. In both cases, I use the medical terms we are learning. There are lots of Greek and Latin root words used in our terminology. For instance, emia means presence of blood, so you have words like anemia or hypervolemia. Learning the roots and prefixes and suffixes helps.

How are you learning the language of your profession?

I have to study for hours on a daily basis. I can't make mistakes in my responses to questions from my peers or my professors. Doctors have to be accurate in the language they use. Medical terminology is extensive and specific. I reference medical dictionaries all the time. I couldn't read medical books if I didn't study. I also read and listen for the language. I can learn some of it that way. I also see how the terms are used in healthcare conversations.

Do you use different language or phrases in different situations (for example, when writing to a doctor vs. writing to other people you work with in clinical practice)?

Yes, I use different language for different situations. For example, when I communicate with patients in the clinic, I have to clarify many of the medical terms by explaining in layman's terms. I might use the term ketone when talking to a fellow medical student or doctor, but when I'm sharing something about ketone with a patient, I'd have to explain that it's a chemical the body makes when there's not enough insulin in the blood.

The phrases I use with patients are more explanatory because I have to clarify the medical terms.

As you notice from this question-response interaction with Chris, his underlying message is that he is using what he learned in school but transferring the learning to new situations. For example, in his initial response he talks about *labeling and annotating sketches, as it* seems that this is the new **genre** he is crafting. In his second response, he refers to writing to med students using a casual style. He is addressing **audience** and **tone.** Did you notice that in several of his responses he described his use of specific **language** and his attention to **language?**

Analyze Interviews.

Although students can't be exposed to the language used in every profession, Mr. Souza attempts to develop their sensitivity to language and the reality that there will be a common base of language used within any work community just like there is in any family or social community. He has students complete an *interview analysis* using the template shown in Figure 3.6; you can download a template from the online companion, resources.corwin.com/ClassroomToCareer.

To guide students to dig deeper into language study using the interviews, he has them record summary data of their own interviews and then exchange data with two other students in class. To complete the analysis, each student identifies what's similar and what's different about each category, then they discuss what they've uncovered. Students are prepared to engage in this collaborative sharing because they have had prior opportunities to collaboratively converse. The text in italics in Figure 3.6 provides an example of what students might fill in based on the interview with Chris Brant.

Example student interview of a young professional, Moriah Makeda

https://docs.google
.com/document/d/lELlu
GRPwrjl5oVl598xwemJH
vfEealMD9M6ZoaYZsEg/
edit?usp=sharing

Figure 3.6 • Interview Analysis Guide Example

	My Interview	My Partner's	What's Similar	What's Different
Profession	*medical student*	*marketing expert, at a content production studio*	*both are careers*	*one person is a student in a technical profession and the other is working in a profession as an employee*
Type of Writing	*detailed notes, with medical terms*	*emails, guideline documents, presentation deck, wrap report, internal chat*	*both use writing in short, abbreviated forms on occasion*	*one uses notes for himself with a personal format; the other uses industry styles of writing*

(Continued)

(Continued)

	My Interview	My Partner's	What's Similar	What's Different
Topics	important medical topics discussed in professor lectures and diagrams	client updates, internal documents	both have a narrow focus on topics within the specific area of interest (medicine and marketing)	one focuses on a wide array of topics in medicine; the other uses industry formats to communicate to various audiences (internal colleagues and clients)
Special terms or words used	sometimes clarification of medical terms is needed; explanations of technical terms are needed for a wider patient audience	industry terms, branded, non-branded, deck— there are lots of terms that we use, especially internally; with clients we explain in details so they understand	both have very specific terms	one has a huge array of medical terms rooted in Latin; the other has industry terms that seem to be more modern
How to learn the language of the profession or job	study medical books and listen to professionals	watching, listening, and communicating— there is no handbook	both require learning the language of the profession	in a medical profession, there are lots of resources, including books and manuals to learn the language; in marketing, language is learned on the job
How language is different in different situations	when talking with medical student peers, professors, or doctors, technical terms and phrases can be used, but when sharing with patients, explanations are needed for terminology	there are one-on-one updates, project manager updates, and internal update; the marketer uses different phrases and styles with each of these types of communication	both have to sometimes convey ideas to laypeople	one has to explain medical terms, conditions, and illnesses using the proper terms, but with examples; the other uses charts, bullet points, and diagrams to explain to various people

online
resources

Mr. Sousza often gives his students opportunities to partner talk about ideas and information they are collecting or creating. Each time they partner chat, he reminds them to not pay attention to just the ideas or information being shared, but to also consider the language and style the speaker is using to convey the message. His purpose is to ensure that his students realize that the language being used to convey the message is as equally important as the message.

Students can use the interview analysis guide in Figure 3.6 to notice similarities and differences in writing given interview responses, as they talk to peers. The benefit of this guide is twofold: Students pay attention to language variations and they engage in focused conversations around language. The example in Figure 3.6 shows the record of two students who documented the similarities and differences around writing in two professions (medical student and marketer, in this example). Students can complete their own chart as they discuss what they have learned about workplace writing by interviewing two different people working in different professions.

Tips for Successful Partner Talk

- Plan in lessons where partner talk should occur.

- Write questions ahead of time, ranging from basic fact-level to deeper thinking and opinion questions.

- Model how to face each other, maintain eye contact, and provide wait time.

- Circulate among students during partner talk to be sure pairs are taking turns listening, talking, and moving from just questioning to conversing.

- Offer suggestions as needed.

- Assess by asking students to reflect on their conversation and to write what they have concluded, learned, and are questioning.

THEIR TURN: INTERVIEWING PROFESSIONALS

Have students interview a person working in a profession about their experiences in writing. Interview questions could include:

- What is your profession?

- What kind of writing do you do in your profession?

- When you write to your work colleagues or your clients, what are the topics you discuss?

- Are there special words or terms you use?

- How are you learning the language of your profession?

- Do you use different language styles, terms, or phrases in different situations (for example, when writing to a coworker vs. writing to other people you work with like clients)?

After each student records notes around their interview, have them work with a partner to share what they've learned and to explore similarities and differences in professions. Students should use the Interview Analysis Guide to record their conversation notes (refer again to Figure 3.6; download the printable from resources.corwin.com/ClassroomToCareer).

Dissect a Writing Artifact.

Mr. Souza asks each student to *dissect* a writing artifact provided by the interviewee. Medical student Chris Brant has provided his annotated study notes (Figure 3.7). As he says, "I'm a medical student. I spend part of my life in hospitals and clinics, and part studying. I suspect I'll continue to be a learner as I move forward in this profession. I've fine-tuned my notetaking skills because they are an important part of the writing I have to do to be successful."

Figure 3.7 • Chris's Writing Artifact: Notes for a Med School Class

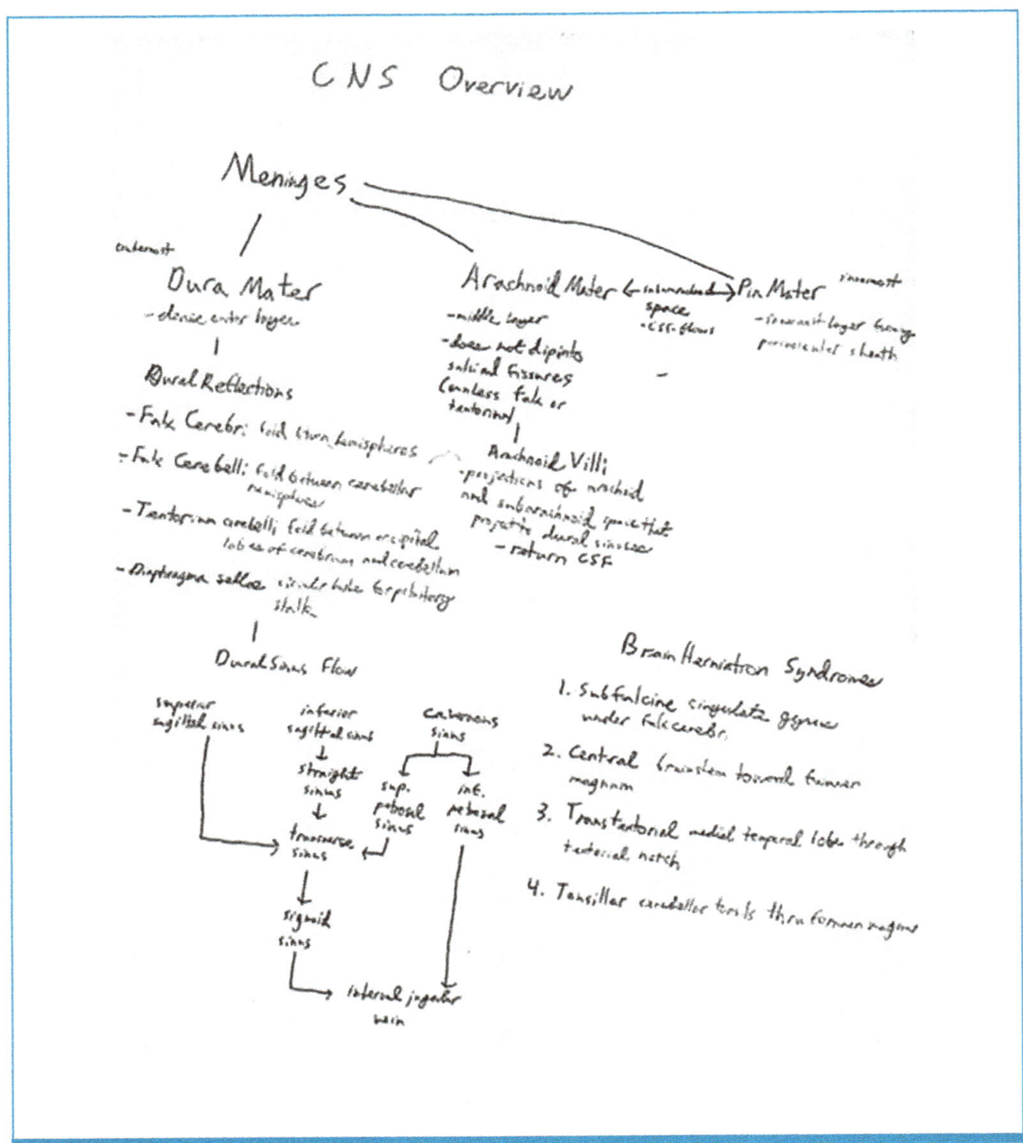

Moriah Makeda has provided a document that she's been working on for a project. Moriah indicates, "My writing has bullet points and lists. To some people, it looks like code, but to my co-workers, it's the usual form of communication. We have our own lingo!" Figure 3.8 shows Moriah's document, a plan for a shade tree project.

Shade Tree Project
Product brief

PROJECT OVERVIEW

Produce a 30s video to support the greening of main street campaign. The project goals are to bring forth awareness and intent to support the mission of the Shade Tree Project. We'll be running this video on a social media platform as a skippable ad, to drive brand goals for Shade Tree.

OBJECTIVE

Motivate viewers to think about the beauty and function of shade trees on main street. When they are looking for a worthwhile project to support, we want them to think about the value of trees to people, especially children, and to think about how trees help to clean the air, provide shade, and increase the value of a neighborhood.

Business objective:
- Increase donations – measured by number of views and contribution amounts.

Marketing objectives:
- Aided awareness of tree benefits to humans and the environment in neighborhoods
- Comprehension of how to support Shade Tree
- Completion of donation process

Creative objectives:
- Humorous
- Relatable
- Grabs attention (i.e. Low skip rate)
- Multiple views by same viewers
- Draws on emotions
- Eye opening
- Causes action

Mr. Souza asks students to dissect a writing artifact, and he models how to do it using a think-aloud technique. He articulates how to consider various aspects of the writing—in other words, he lets students hear his thinking around Moriah's writing. Mr Souza's think-aloud starts like this:

> Now students, I have Ms. Makeda's writing here on the document camera and you have a copy to view as well. I'm going to show you how I think about this writing artifact. I'm going to dissect it to notice phrases, academic terms, literary devices, and unique words. I'm focused on the language of this document, and I'll record this on my dissection chart.

Mr. Souza provides a *Dissect a Document* chart to students (see Figure 3.9; a downloadable version is found online at resources.corwin.com/ ClassroomToCareer). He prompts students to notice and jot down phrases, academic terms, literary devices, and unique words. Mr. Souza's think-aloud is designed to show students how to identify these elements. They even have a literary device guide to help them with their dissection (see Figure 3.10). Mr. Souza continues:

> I notice that this document has a couple of paragraphs listed at the top. These seem to introduce the plan for the Shade Tree project by providing the overview and the objective. There are lots of bullet point lists. I think this makes the proposal easy to follow. I know this project plan is for Shade Tree because it's named at the top. That must be the company name. This is a very concise, straightforward document, so I'm not expecting to see many literary devices, but I'm still going to look. Oh, I do see some parallel structure in the sentence, "When they are looking for a worthwhile project to support, we want them to think about the value of trees to people, especially children, and to think about how trees help to clean the air, provide shade, and increase the value of a neighborhood." That last part of the sentence has some parallelism, "to think about how trees help to clean the air, provide shade, and increase the value of a neighborhood." The tone is businesslike mostly, but friendly. I can tell it's written for colleagues to read at a business site. It's their project plan. As I noticed before, the objectives of the project are clearly stated at the top of the page.

Figure 3.9 • Dissect a Document Example (based on Moriah's writing)

Elements to notice	What I noticed
Paragraphs	Two at the start
Descriptions	Brief description of project
Bullet points	Several lists with bullet points for business objectives, marketing objectives, and creative objectives
Lists	List in bulleted form
Letter structure	no
Company name or logo	Yes – Shade Tree
Literary devices	Parallelism – ". . . to think about how trees help to clean the air, provide shade, and increase the value of a neighborhood."
Tone	Friendly but businesslike
Humor	Not a focus
Illustrations, charts, data tables, graphs	none

Figure 3.10 • Literary Devices Quick Guide

Literary Devices	Meaning	Examples	What's in my Text
Alliteration	A number of words, having the same first consonant sound, occur close together in a series	The twine was tightly tied.	
Antithesis	Two opposite ideas are put together in a sentence to achieve a contrasting effect	"To err is human; to forgive divine." – Alexander Pope	
Epithet	Describes a place, a thing, or a person in such a way that it helps in making its characteristics more prominent than they actually are	"I've come, As you surmise, with comrades on a ship, Sailing across the wine-dark sea to men Whose style of speech is very different . . ." —*The Odyssey* (by Homer)	
Hyperbole	A figure of speech that involves an exaggeration of ideas for the sake of emphasis	"I had to wait in the station for ten days—an eternity." —*The Heart of Darkness* (by Joseph Conrad)	
Metaphor	Compares two things by stating one is the other	"'Life,' wrote a friend of mine, 'is a public performance on the violin, in which you must learn the instrument as you go along.'" —*A Room With a View* (by E.M. Forster)	
Onomatopoeia	Words that imitate the sound they describe	Plunk, crash, pop	
Oxymoron	Two words that create a paradox	Alone together Deafening silence	
Parallelism	Words or phrases with a similar structure	I came home from school, studied for a test, and had dinner with my family.	
Simile	Compares one object to another	"I wandered lonely as a cloud that floats on high o'er vales and hills." —"The Daffodils" (by William Wordsworth)	
Understatement	Makes an idea less important than it is	"I have to have this operation. It isn't very serious. I have this tiny little tumor on the brain." —*Catcher in the Rye* (by J. D. Salinger)	
Other literary devices?			

After Mr. Souza finishes his think-aloud, he lets students practice their own text dissections, with work emails, blog posts, project proposals, newscast scripts, college essays, notes, and even supply order documents. The array of writing is wide and deep. Mr. Souza wants his students to see many possibilities for writing beyond high school.

THEIR TURN: DISSECTING A WORKPLACE ARTIFACT

Provide students with a workplace document, such as the memorandum provided in Figure 3.11. Invite students to examine the document and then use the Dissect a Document Chart to analyze it. Be sure to model first.

Figure 3.11 • Memo for an Environmental Impact Report

Big Tree Engineering Company

Memorandum

To: James MacIntosh
From: Michelle Machado
CC: Carolina Jones

Introduction
The environmental impact survey is planned for the plot of land at the location Fifth Avenue and Elm Street.

Materials and Methods
Survey and data collection will be used to conduct an impact report in light of the proposed construction of a new library on the plot of land located at this intersection.

Results
Data will include calibration curves and calculations. Raw data and field notes will be provided in the appendices.

Discussion
This assessment will include a review of the impact on the local environment, construction impacts, building design, and post-construction operational impacts. An overall assessment of these factors will be discussed in the survey report.

Conclusion
This study will present data to clarify the impacts of construction on this delicate natural environment, located on the edge of an important forest ecosystem.

1219 MARCUS STREET, WINSTON, CA
T 215- 333-7812 U

Composing With Language and Voice in Mind

Once students have learned to look at language within a text, it's important to have them practice writing for various purposes and in various ways using language register and variety. RAFT—R stands for Role, A for Audience, F for Format, and T for Topic—is a valuable way to get students to write for various purposes to different audiences. Students should consider the kind of language—register and variety—as they compose their RAFT. Consider the example RAFTs in Figure 3.12 for your students. What other RAFTS might you offer?

Figure 3.12 • Examples of RAFT planning

Role	Audience	Format	Topic
Marketing creative	Your team	Proposal document	Our campaign for a new coffee maker
College student	Professor	Poem	Becoming an adult
Travel blogger	The public	Blog	The best things to see when traveling to your city or town
Restaurant manager	Food supplier	Email	Order these foods
Reporter	Readers of your newspaper	Short news brief	What happened today in . . .
Plumber	Customer	Invoice	Work completed and the cost

THEIR TURN: STUDENT PRACTICE

Once students have a strong grasp on how a writer's text "works" on a language level, they can practice using strategies like RAFT and real-world writing before they apply their skills to a new writing piece.

Choose one of the RAFTs from Figure 3.12 or create a RAFT from your content area. Ask students to write to the designated audience using the format described and the topic indicated. After students compose their writing, they can share their RAFTs with a partner. This helps students see various ways that their peers might write to the target audience about the given topic.

SUM IT UP

Learning how successful writing works by studying language is not a clear-cut, uniform process. It requires closely studying how authors interact with their audiences and paying attention to the language registers and varieties used, as well as to text features like bullet points, figures/graphs, and other key elements. As illustrated by the teacher and student examples in this chapter, much of the heavy lifting of language learning is done in the reading and text dissection phase.

Teaching students to understand language is just one part of guiding them toward more flexibility when writing beyond high school. If students become familiar with both language registers and language varieties, and if they have opportunities to read, analyze, and dissect writing samples, they will be more adept at noticing language elements when they encounter them in the workplace and situations beyond high school. Then they'll be able to compose appropriately for the audience they are targeting.

ANTICIPATION GUIDE

Revisit the anticipation guide that appeared at the beginning of the chapter to check and expand your initial responses. Even if you had the correct answer, now you can add an explanation that illustrates your deepened understanding.

Possible Fact	True	False	What else can you add?
The term *language registers* refers to the degree of formality and informality used to communicate in different situations.	X		
Academic writing centers mostly in standard language, so it is best to teach students using a model in standard English.		X	Students should study a variety of texts because they will be expected to write for a variety of audiences. Privileging one type of writing over another without attention to context is limiting.
Students benefit more from writing tasks designed within the context of their discipline rather than those that span multiple content areas.	X		

Structure and Evidence

How Do I Share My Thinking Most Effectively?

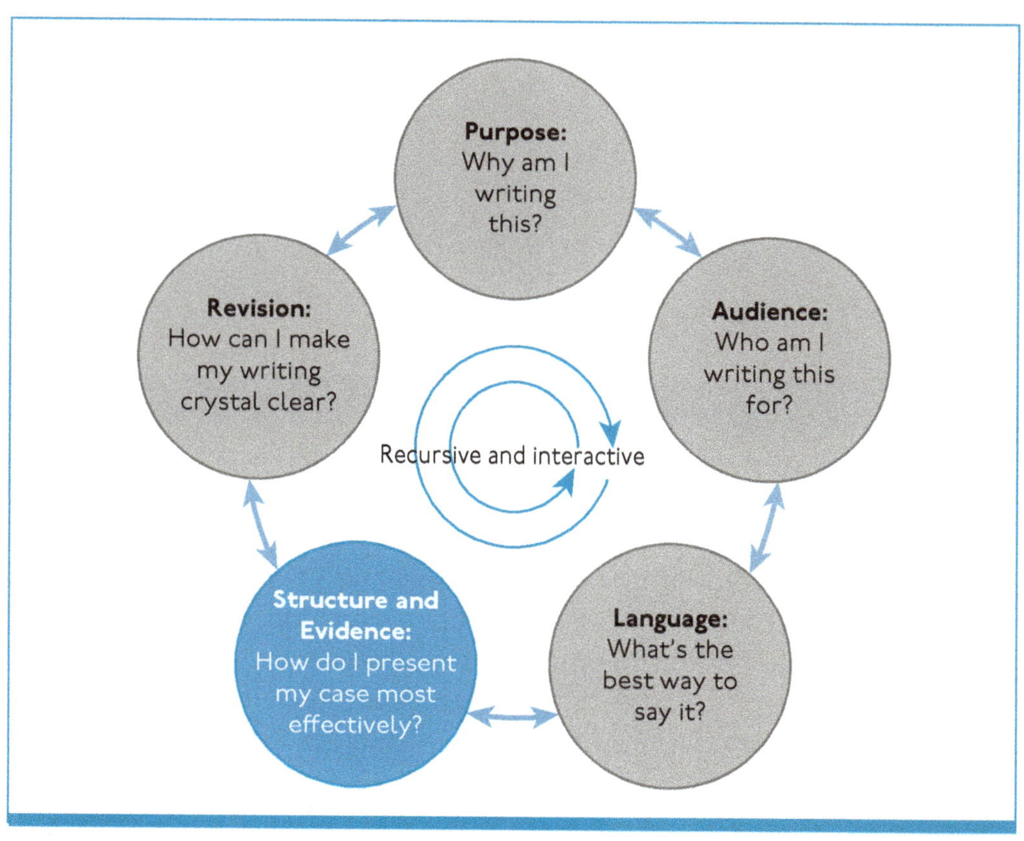

Extraordinary claims require extraordinary evidence.

— Carl Sagan, American scientist, author, and science communicator

ANTICIPATION GUIDE

The focus of this chapter is on *structure and evidence*. Before you begin reading this chapter, stop for a minute to complete the anticipation guide to check your knowledge of the following information that will be shared throughout the chapter. At the conclusion in the *Sum It Up* section, you'll be able to revisit these facts and also self-assess what you've learned.

Use this anticipation guide to assess your beginning understanding:

Anticipation Guide

Possible Fact	True	False
There are three main types of evidence used when writing most texts.		
Rubrics are an effective way to communicate the kinds of structures and evidence you want your students to use.		
Cross-curricular writing projects can encourage real-world application of using evidence and structure for a specific audience.		

We can all think of a time when someone had just the right approach to convince us of something we might normally have opposed. Perhaps it was a savvy salesperson citing the most recent safety ratings for a car we were uncertain about buying, or perhaps it was an emotional appeal for contributions to a particularly heartbreaking GoFundMe campaign. We often select specific approaches and evidence to support our own persuasive endeavors; when consoling a friend over a recent loss, a text message or email may not be as appropriate as a phone call or face-to-face meeting. Conversely, a phone call to a boss or supervisor on vacation with a request to be reimbursed for supplies would most likely *not* be received well. In this chapter, we'll walk through suggestions, teaching tools, and models for teaching students how to use evidence and structure to support their writing in whatever discipline or career path they pursue.

WHAT ARE EVIDENCE AND STRUCTURE?

The art of argumentation and persuasion requires a knowledge of audience and context and the ability to tailor or structure and support one's message appropriately for the situation. We make these decisions daily in our personal lives without even noticing when we include some details while leaving out others, or when we call a person rather than text. The same type of thinking happens in our professional interactions, and while the manifestations of argument may look different in a scientific laboratory versus a firehouse, the approach is the same. When we make a claim, we think of the most compelling way to support our point, and this largely depends on who we are trying to convince or influence. Sometimes that support comes in the form of hard data like statistics or established scientific studies; other times the best source of evidence comes from first-hand accounts or testimonials. As you've read throughout the chapters of this book, context matters. It follows, then, that our classroom instruction should prepare students to think about how the evidence and format or structure they use have a deliberate connection to *whom* and for *what* purpose they are writing.

Although we may be most used to thinking about supporting our ideas in writing from an ethos (textual), pathos (testimonial), and logos (statistical) perspective, each of these appeals encompasses many different types of evidence. Other ways of supporting our ideas would be using anecdotal, statistical, testimonial, analogical, textual, and hypothetical evidence. Look at Figure 4.1 to learn about and see examples of each type of evidence.

Figure 4.1 • Types of Evidence

Type of evidence	Example(s)
Anecdotal: Using a personal experience to illustrate a point, sometimes shared in a casual or non-systematic manner.	A person relates a story of his phone falling out of his shirt pocket into the toilet to prove that shirt pockets should be deeper.
Statistical: collected, organized, and validated set of information gathered in a precise way, such as graphs, often shared to support a particular position	In a class of students voting on class colors, the colors receiving the most votes would be chosen based on the statistical percentage or evidence of how many students chose a particular color.
Testimonial: written or oral statement given by a person with credible personal knowledge or observational experiences	An interview from a user of a product. A teacher uses examples of a student's work or performance, in addition to her personal knowledge, to support why the student received an excellent semester grade.

(Continued)

(Continued)

Type of evidence	Example(s)
Analogical: Sharing a familiar example to clarify a less-known or new experience	Using recently sold home prices to project a sales price of a similar home. The famous quote from the movie, *Forrest Gump*, "Life is like a box of chocolates—you never know what you're gonna get" is an example of the sharing of a known and new experience.
Textual: quotations from an established piece of work to support your thesis	Examples include, statistics, direct quotations, graphics, or any information taken from a text used to support a claim.
Hypothetical: an imagined, suggested, or not currently true, scenario to illustrate your main point	When someone cautions you to take an umbrella with you just in case it rains, they are hypothesizing a solution that will stop you from getting wet—even if it's not yet raining.

Defining different types of writing structures can be less clear, depending on the purpose, style, and audience of the author. However, a good starting place would be to think about the different basic writing structures we may see in the four main modes of writing: *narrative*, which shares a fictional story experience; *persuasive*, which attempts to convince the reader of something; *expository*, which exposes or explains information; and *descriptive*, which offers the reader a mental rendering or image. Figure 4.2 details common writing structures.

Figure 4.2 • Writing Structures Within the 4 Modes

Narrative	• Common plot structures (like Freytag's pyramid) • Prose or Fiction – *Cinderella*, *The Hunger Games*, *A Raisin In The Sun* • First person accounts, *"The first thing you should know about me is I am my father's son"* from *Red Rising* • Plays, *Romeo & Juliet*, *Hamilton*
Persuasive	• Thesis-driven, multi-paragraph essays • Thesis-driven speeches like Abraham Lincoln's Gettysburg Address • Persuasive letters like Martin Luther King's *Letter From Birmingham Jail* • Op-Eds like "A picture of loneliness: you are looking at the last male northern white rhino" by Jonathan Jones (http://bit.ly/3J9sAui) • Advertisements like the 1984 Apple Computer ad, which is considered one of the most persuasive ever shared (http://bit.ly/3ZTxHpm)

Expository	• Compare/Contrast
	• Scientific papers such as "How Long Is the Coast of Britain?" by Benoit Mandelbrot (https://bit.ly/3LeWSPa)
	• How-to guides or manuals like *Better Homes & Gardens* "butterfly garden" guide (http://bit.ly/3T9DDsk)
Descriptive	• Poems such as "**when you are old**" by William Butler Yeats (http://bit.ly/3yAzrrL)
	• Firsthand accounts such as John Lewis's testimony from a hearing resulting from the March 7, 1965, march from Selma to Montgomery in support of voting rights (http://bit.ly/3FiHwFp)
	• Detailed descriptions

PAUSE AND CONSIDER

Which writing structures do you think your students will encounter most frequently in the workplace? What types of evidence may they use in their workplace writing? Jot down any ideas for how you might integrate more exposure to these structures and revisit these ideas as you read through the chapter:

____

____

____

____

____

WHY SHOULD WE FOCUS ON UNDERSTANDING EVIDENCE AND STRUCTURE?

For firefighter-paramedic Tom Erikson, writing might seem a surprising aspect of his job. Any time a patient requires CPR, refuses treatment, or passes away, Mr. Erikson must write a report of the incident using specific details and protocol for a target audience. "My write-ups are used for a variety of purposes and audiences," Mr. Erikson notes, "so I have to be sure that I am considering the readers while still accurately depicting the events of the incident." Because so many different readers will access this document—anyone from the hospital workers who provide the care to the patient in question, to insurance companies, and even to potential judges and jurors, should a lawsuit arise—Mr. Erikson has his work cut out for him in an environment that isn't always conducive to writing. For his audience and writing purpose, accuracy and objectivity are key.

Mr. Erikson points out, "It is important that I report only the facts. Any emotion or judgment I include in the report distracts from the accuracy of the report and can actually make me look less credible. I try to stay as objective as I can and include pertinent details that will help the reader understand what happened. For example, if an elderly person refuses treatment, I will be especially sure to note whether they experienced a fall or loss of consciousness, which are risk factors for that demographic." For paramedic Erikson, he must consider the objective of the report—to convey the facts—while considering who will be reading the narrative and which of those facts are especially pertinent. "While I was in paramedic school, we were taught to remember the acronym 'OPQRST,' which helps me make sure I am including all of the correct information that my audience will want to know." See Figure 4.3 for a detailed explanation of each component.

Figure 4.3 • What Is OPQRST?

Onset	When did the issue occur? What was the patient doing at the time of onset? Did it come all at once, or was onset gradual?
Provocation	Is there anything that aggravates the symptoms? Makes them better?
Quality	Describe in detail the pain (for example, *squeezing, sharp, dull*, etc.)
Region	Does the pain stay in one place or move (radiate)?
Severity	What is the pain on a rating level of 1–10 (10 being unbearable)?
Time	When did the illness present symptoms?

Adapted from Baker (2014).

For Mr. Erikson's purpose, he focuses on writing a short, objective summary of the event, with times and accurate descriptions whenever possible. Mr. Erikson also uses abbreviations and language known to his readers. See Figure 4.4 for an example of the six points illustrating how firefighter-paramedic Erikson and those in similar lines of work might use as a guide as they complete an incident report.

Here's his thinking: "Since my audience are people who know the 'lingo,' I keep my notes abbreviated when possible yet include all elements of the event that would help tell exactly what occurred," Mr. Erikson notes.

"This report not only serves to facilitate patient care, but also protects me from liability if a patient should claim I did something incorrectly. So, it's really important that my writing be clear, objective, and professional—nothing too ancillary or emotional." Figure 4.4 provides an example of how Firefighter Erikson might compose a narrative for his job, paying particular attention to the type of evidence he provides in his narrative, as well as how it is presented. Notice that his notes contain specific details that can be presented as evidence to support the claim as well as a potential structure that his narrative might follow.

Figure 4.4 • Paramedic Notes Example

As you read this chart, you will notice many abbreviations that are used by medical professionals during notetaking and reporting. This discourse is learned during training.*

Audience	Medical professionals, medical billing companies, health insurance, receiving hospital, ER personnel, lawyers/jurists/judges	
Incident	• Brief details (time on scene, location, how patient was found)	M65698 Dispatched to a private residence for a medical aid at 12:45 hours. U/A at 1325, pt sitting on the couch in a supine position. Pt's spouse met us at door.
Chief complaint	• Age, gender, main complaint of patient • Commentary/information from bystanders (use quotation marks)	57 Y/O M C/O of tightness in Cx (tightness in chest) and SOB (shortness of breath). Pt's spouse states, "Todd was putting something in the rafters when he grasped his Cx and complained of feeling a heaviness." Pt states, "The pain is not unbearable but really uncomfortable; my Cx feels tight and I can't get a full breath in."
History	• Short narrative of events leading to illness • Mechanism of injury (MOI), if applicable • SAMPLE (Signs/Symptoms, Allergies, Medications, Pertinent Medical History, Last oral intake, Events leading up)	Pt states, "I felt a sudden, dull pain in my Cx and couldn't get a breath, so I stopped what I was doing and came inside to sit down." Pt C/O Cx tightness and SOB. (-) to any numbness or tingling. Not taking any Rx other than OTC multivitamins qdxl. No known allergies.
Assessment	• <u>AVPU</u> and <u>OPQRST</u> • (Alert, alert to Verbal, alert to Pain, Unresponsive) • (Onset, Provocation/Palliation, Quality, Radiation/ Region/ Reoccurrence, Severity, Time) • Important findings and results of physical exam • Vital signs	Appx. 1330, B/P 140/100, P 72, RR 23. Skin is pale, cool and diaphoretic. HEENT: C/O dizziness, (-) ear, neck, throat or eye pain. No evidence of trauma. Cx has equal rise/ fall, L/S clear bilaterally, C/O dull chest pain. The pain started when pt was lifting heavy item into rafters and feels heavier when pt breathes in. Pain radiates out to entire Cx. Pain is 7/10 and started at appx. 1115. Abd is soft, non-tender and no masses. Pelvis is intact and no pain

(Continued)

(Continued)

Audience	Medical professionals, medical billing companies, health insurance, receiving hospital, ER personnel, lawyers/jurists/judges	
Treatment	• List of treatment in chronological order	Appx. 1231, pt placed on 02 @ 15lpm via NRB and IV 18G to L AC. Administered ASA 162mg chewable PO, NTG 0.4mg SL, and NTG ointment 1" to L Cx. ECG Sinus tach @ 104 and stable. Pt transferred from dining room to gurney with assistance and Tx to Memorial Medical Center. Pt's spouse followed in POV.
Transport	• Why the patient required transportation by ambulance • Where the patient was transported and if any changes were noted en route	Emergency Tx was necessary because pt is suspected to have a possible MI. Contacted Memorial Medical Center to notify them of pt's arrival and condition. No changes to pt's condition en route. Pt care was transferred to Jane Doe, RN at Memorial Medical Center at appx. 1301

Adapted from Baker (2014).

*Note that the table shows the parts of the account, which is written out in paragraph form for the actual paramedic report.

YOUR TURN: USING RUBRICS

Mr. Erikson knows his audience, his purpose, and what they want to see to provide the best care, decisions, and outcomes for patients and other stakeholders. Likewise, teachers should provide structured opportunities for their students to systematically evaluate who they are writing for and in which context before they decide what kind of evidence they should use. This can be done by providing a rubric that directs student attention to these elements. For example, you might introduce the concept of using audience and purpose to guide evidence selection by using a workplace example like Mr. Erikson's to show how professionals tailor their writing to a set of criteria. By demonstrating the relationship between the paramedic notes (Figure 4.4) and the acronym Mr. Erikson learned during his training (Figure 4.3), you would be modeling how rubrics work in a professional setting. Using this career connection, you might present a rubric that you use in your course, highlighting the practice of using a rubric to guide academic writing to Mr. Erikson's workplace example.

A classroom-friendly iteration of Mr. Erikson's thinking can be represented by the following points on the Purpose-Driven Writing Rubric from Chapter One (see Figure 1.7 and online companion), which includes the following points:

I have demonstrated knowledge of my audience by:

- My word choice (I have used language that is appropriate to my audience).

- My use of evidence (I have included examples, illustrations, and other artifacts that will best convince my audience).

- My tone (I have made certain stylistic choices to further my purpose with my audience).

- My formatting choices (I have considered the structure and associated features that best suit my purpose and audience).

HOW DO WE TEACH STUDENTS TO THINK ABOUT STRUCTURE AND EVIDENCE WHEN THEY WRITE?

Using "Expert Projects" to Teach How to Select Evidence

Thanks to the state standards, most students know by a very young age they need to support their claims with evidence. However, many students see evidence collection as a task to be checked off on the rubric rather than a thoughtful enterprise that makes or breaks purpose-driven writing. Just as we witnessed with Mr. Erikson, artfully chosen evidence and well-crafted structure in a piece of writing reflect an author's depth of understanding of their audience. For students to be truly successful in their writing endeavors and develop the type of critical thinking required to succeed out of the classroom, they must see the inextricable link between who they are writing for, what topic they are writing about, what information they will share, and what structure they will use to accomplish their intent.

For Ava Hollins's students, this knowledge is developed through an "expert project." For many years, her students only approached audience-driven writing in their English courses via long-term inquiries using an adaptation of Jim Burke's model she learned about in a district-wide professional development (Burke, 2018; Roberts, 2014). Her colleague Tony Meyers, a chemistry teacher, expressed wanting to take on a similar project, but using scientific inquiry and writing as the focus. Many schools have iterations of this, and Ms. Hollins and Mr. Meyers decided to collaborate on a project that taught literacy skills across content areas. For their new and improved approach, students took on a scientific question in Mr. Meyers' class versus just a topic of interest and learned how to apply science-specific research skills to the writing process. (The online companion contains a detailed example of The Expert Project outline and instructions Ms. Hollins and Mr. Meyers created.)

To complete the assignment, students select a topic related to a scientific question they would like to answer or explore for an audience of fellow scientists. To help emphasize the focus on text structure and evidence, Ms. Hollins and Mr. Meyers limit their instruction to scientific papers and research so students can see how the specific purpose and audience of their work will require close attention to how they present and organize their work. Students then go through a series of lessons, taught both in science and English class, where they examine model texts and learn about how they work, formulate a hypothesis for the question they want to explore, then conduct scholarly research related to their questions. See the Expert Project Planner in Figure 4.5 for a detailed view of this project (download the template from the online companion, resources.corwin.com/ ClassroomToCareer).

Figure 4.5 • Expert Project Planner

Phase of research	Questions to consider	Product/Success Criteria
Step 1: Find your Big Question	What is something I have been wondering about? What makes me curious about how the world works?	A focused, researchable question *Do all citizens still have equal voting rights in the United States regardless of race, color, condition, or servitude as guaranteed by Amendments 15 and 19? Or are voting rights being covertly revoked by gerrymandering, in-person voting requirements, and limited hours for voting?*
Step 2: Formulate a hypothesis	What do I think is a reasonable answer to my proposed question? What do I think my research will reveal?	A hypothesis ("if . . . then . . .") *I think my research might reveal that if the actions of gerrymandering, in-person voting requirements, and limited voting hours are in place, then the voting rights of certain citizens are not equal. This situation would have ramifications for political outcomes.*
Step 3: Assess current knowledge and conduct preliminary research	What do I already know? What do I need to know? What is considered a reputable source in science? What does a scientific paper/ article look like?	Annotated bibliography using peer-reviewed articles and experiments formatted in APA (at least four sources) Scientific paper "dissection"

Phase of research	Questions to consider	Product/Success Criteria
Step 4: Reassess knowledge and conduct deeper research	What do I know now? What holes in my knowledge do I still have? What alternate sources of evidence and research can I find? (example: interviews, self-conducted research, etc.)	Additional sources (two to three more) in annotated bibliography A short narrative "check-in" about challenges and successes in the research process
Step 5: Constructing a Scientific Research Paper	How is a scientific paper organized? What evidence should I include and where? Has my hypothesis been proven or disproven?	Finished paper with evidence of revision/editing. Sections to include: Abstract Introduction Methods Results Discussion/Conclusion
Step 6: Use your research to persuade: Public Rhetoric Campaign	Who needs to know about the research I conducted? What do I want them to believe? What information do they need to know?	Completed "Checklist for writing" + finished product (varies depending on student)

online resources

After students have completed Steps 1 and 2 in the Expert Project Planner, Ms. Hollins teaches her class, through modeling and closely reading multiple scientific research papers, how professional science papers are structured and written, to assist them in Step 3. More specifically, Ms. Hollins models how to investigate a research question through reading texts that address aspects of a topic. Before beginning to guide students through a close reading of a science text related to a research question, Ms. Hollins models how to notice aspects of text to identify the research format. In this case, her research question is about kelp forests and ocean acidification. Here's an excerpt of Ms. Hollins's think-aloud of the text *Stanford Researchers Explore Potential for Kelp to Relieve Ocean Acidification* (Torrent Tucker, 2020, see http://bit.ly/3ZH8rDc):

> Since my research question is *Can growing and maintaining kelp forests help with the problems related to global climate change?*, I'm going to take a look at a few articles that are rooted in research around this topic. This first article is titled "Stanford Researchers Explore Potential for Kelp to Relieve Ocean Acidification." The title is revealing. Since the researchers are looking at the potential of kelp for reducing ocean acidification, I think this concept is new and not yet implemented. Now I'll start reading. *"Ethereal, swaying pillars of brown kelp along California's coasts grow up through*

> *the water column, culminating in a dense surface canopy of thick fronds that provide homes and refuge for numerous marine creatures. There's speculation that these giant algae may protect coastal ecosystems by helping alleviate acidification caused by too much atmospheric carbon being absorbed by the seas."* I can see that I'm on the right track with this article—it relates to my research question. I'm hoping that the article will explain a bit more about ocean acidification, as I'm not sure I understand the problem.

Ms. Hollins continues thinking aloud about the paragraph, then shifts her thinking to pay attention to the structure of the text, so that students understand how important it is to notice the structure of a science research article:

> As I skim the headings, I can see how this article evolves. The first heading says, *Why kelp?* This is where the author clarifies the problem. She writes, *One of the detrimental impacts of increased carbon in the atmosphere is its subsequent absorption by the planet's oceans, which causes acidification—a chemical imbalance that can negatively impact the overall health of marine ecosystems, including animals people depend on for food.* The next heading is called *Designing a nature-based solution* and is followed by text that describes the possible solution called "blue carbon." The last heading is called *A model for future study.* In this section I see that the researchers have developed a model and feel that future research could clarify the solutions to the problem of ocean acidification more clearly. There's a structure here — problem, solution, next steps for future study.

Ms. Hollins finishes her think-aloud and then tells students they will be engaging in a close reading so that they can dig deeper with a text and so that they can identify the structure of the text.

To explicitly connect this writing with the public rhetoric unit happening in their English courses, Ms. Hollins and Mr. Tony Meyers, the English teacher, have agreed to make this a joint persuasive research paper aimed at a specific audience of the student's choosing. When they reach Step 6, students will take the information they gathered during the scientific inquiry portion of the assignment and begin to tailor that information to a specific audience. At this point in the writing process—like firefighter-paramedic Erikson did—students have identified their topic, audience, and purpose.

Now they are at the phase of writing in which they are choosing how they are going to present their topic to a specific audience. Take a look at Figure 4.6 below to see how students have begun to deliberately plot out how they will write to the audience they have identified.

THEIR TURN: IDENTIFYING APPROPRIATE EVIDENCE

Have students practice completing the chart in Figure 4.5, which you can download from resources.corwin.com/ClassroomToCareer. In this example, Steps 1 and 2 have been completed by a student in Mr. Meyers's class (italics). Have students finish completing this or start a new one on a topic they choose.

Ms. Hollins advises her class that they will use their research from a prior annotated bibliography assignment and scientific research paper to support their creation of an audience-specific text. "Remember," she says, "when a lawyer is in the courtroom arguing a case, she doesn't present *all* of her evidence—she only includes what is most important and persuasive." For Ms. Hollins's and Mr. Meyers's students, the lesson is centered around how to choose the most compelling evidence and writing strategies for the audience at hand. They also both make sure to highlight the differences between a scientific research paper and a public rhetoric piece: in a scientific research paper, the purpose is to inform in the most unbiased, evidence-based manner possible; in a public rhetoric piece, however, there is an underlying thread of persuasion. The form and content decisions in Steps 1 through 5 (see again Figure 4.5) are driven by the purpose and the norms and values of the scientific community.

Step 6 invites students to reimagine the information they have and approach it differently; their learning becomes dynamic, and they must shift their concept of what type of evidence is appropriate. Go ahead and have students compare Figures 4.4 and 4.5 to see the crossover between Ms. Hollins's and Mr. Meyers's graphic organizer and the type of incident report a firefighter, paramedic, police officer, or other public servant in the field might fill out. Just as Mr. Erikson from the fire department knows what details and evidence his readers want to see, these students know what their intended audience needs to know in order for their text to be successful.

This time Mr. Meyers thinks aloud to show students how he would consider the audience when composing a persuasive text. He goes back to the "kelp" topic that Ms. Hollins used to model reading research and noticing structure:

First, I'm going to identify my purpose for writing. I'm going to address several potential donors who are looking for ways to invest in efforts that reduce the negative effects of climate change. I want to persuade them to invest in kelp forest restoration as a natural way to offset carbon emissions. I'm going to have to start with an explanation of the problem. Then I'll move to the effectiveness of kelp forests as a "blue carbon" solution. Since I know that they are interested in donations related to solutions to climate change, I will present the science aspects of my solution, with a tone that is professional yet friendly. I'll share my ideas using a problem/solution structure. Also, I'll include headings to help orient the donors who are reading this request. After I share the science part of the problem and the solution, I'll shift to persuading my readers that kelp forests are better than other means of reducing carbon, like terrestrial forests. I remember that one of the texts I read had information around that persuasive idea. This will be the evidence I need to convince them that kelp reforestation is worthy of their donations.

After thinking aloud to showcase how to shift from research writing to persuasive writing that uses research, Mr. Meyers tasks students with thinking about their persuasive writing process. To support their thinking, he shares the graphic organizer called *Planning Your Structure and Evidence for an Audience*. Figure 4.6 shows an example based on Mr. Meyers' reading and think-aloud; you can download a blank version for student use from the companion website, resources.corwin.com/ ClassroomToCareer.

Figure 4.6 • Planning Your Structure and Evidence for an Audience

Purpose of text:	**Why should people know about your topic?** Kelp forest restoration is worth investing in because it's a natural way to combat carbon emissions.
Audience of text:	**Style connected to your audience (tone, type of language, perspective):** I need to have a friendly, yet professional tone. I need to convey a sense of urgency—it's important to act now, because carbon emissions are negatively affecting global climate. **Structure of text (cause/effect, etc.):** I'll start with cause/effect when I share about carbon emissions and the effects on climate. Then I'll move to problem/solution text structure when I talk about how kelp forests capture and store atmospheric carbon. **Features of text (headers, columns, images, etc.):** I'll use bold print headers for main ideas (kelp forests capture and store carbon) and will add photos of beautiful kelp forests to contrast with photos of cars and factories emitting carbon gases.

Strategy #1	**What type of evidence/writing will you provide to support this strategy?** **Explain the cause and effect issue:** Ocean acidification results from too much carbon being dissolved in the oceans. The carbon comes from burning fossil fuels. According to Tucker, increasing pH of seawater is the "harmful fallout from climate change on marine ecosystems and the food they produce for human populations."
Strategy #2	**What type of evidence/writing will you provide to support this strategy?** **Talk about the problem/solution:** Kelp grows fast. During the growing process, carbon is removed from the seawater where the kelp lives. This reduces pH of the water.
Strategy #3	**What type of evidence/writing will you provide to support this strategy?** **Discuss why investments are needed:** We need funds to support kelp farming, so that we can reduce the harmful outcomes associated with global climate change.

THEIR TURN: PLANNING FOR EVIDENCE-BASED WRITING

Ask your students to practice planning to write for an audience using the Planning Your Structure and Evidence for an Audience graphic organizer from Figure 4.6. You can provide them with a topic or have them select a topic. Here are a few suggestions: *cooking should be taught in middle school and high school; there are solutions to unsustainable fast fashion; nutrition programs should consider culture and traditions.* Students will need a little background knowledge to practice thinking about purpose, audience, and evidence, but remember, this is a practice activity. For a more detailed writing task, students should invest more time in researching a topic through wide reading.

PAUSE AND CONSIDER

How can you leverage your colleagues to provide cross-curricular opportunities for students to explore evidence and text structures (or other aspects of the writing process) in career documents and purposes? Revisit these ideas as you learn more about our featured teachers in the rest of the chapters and review those from the previous chapters to flesh out your thinking.

____

____

____

____

____

____

Teaching Text Structures and Features

Though an integral component to a successful piece of text, structure is often overlooked in the writing process, with text features, a significant component of structure, trailing behind. Sometimes, as in firefighter-paramedic Erikson's case, a certain structure and associated features like headers and captions are mandated by an institution, whereas in other situations, the form of the text follows the function of it. For Ms. Hollins and Mr. Meyers, it is important to provide multiple opportunities for their students to see how authors structure their texts in a way that shows intention and alignment with audience and purpose. To frontload this part of the eventual writing process, Ms. Hollins and Mr. Meyers spent considerable time using model texts to teach structure and text features. They read a mix of informational and argumentative texts with a variety of structures and features to help their students internalize the relationship between audience, purpose, and structure. Ms. Hollins and Mr. Meyers created a revised version of the graphic organizer from Chapter 1 (Figure 1.3) to help their students look at the structure of a text and its connection to a texts' purpose and readership. In this organizer (see Figure 4.7) students examine the structures and features that drive an argument so they can understand how they work and then begin to incorporate similar moves and thinking into their own writing.

Figure 4.7 • Planning Text Features

Purpose of text: to clarify the benefits of driving an electric car **Overall text structure:** There are bullet points at the start of the article to highlight the main topics discussed in the article. The headings indicate that concerns of owning an electric car are addressed (popularity, price, range running costs, charging, etc). There's an easy-to-read chart that shows cost, range, and charge time for different EVs. There are links to related articles (small EVs, best seven-seater, etc. There are also nice photos of cars throughout the article.	**Textual evidence (where did you find the purpose?):** The title of the article and the bullet points at the start of the article identify the purpose.
Feature #1 Headings	**Textual evidence. Where is it? What does it do?** The headings help the reader to navigate the text. They let the reader know what the upcoming section will be about. The headings in this article address concerns that many people have about EVs, like cost, driving range, and charging times.
Feature #2 Chart	**Textual evidence. Where is it? What does it do?** The chart shows comparisons of cars, including Honda, Fiat, and others. The comparisons are for charge cost, cost per mile, range, and other areas of interest. The chart shows the value of an EV and helps consumers see their options.
Feature #3 Photos	**Textual evidence. Where is it? What does it do?** There are numerous color photos of cars. They are attractive shots showing cars parked in beautiful locations, driving along seaside highways, and even plugged in and charging. The photos showcase the visual appeal of EV cars.
How did the structures and features of the text further its purpose? Write below, using Claim, Evidence, and Reasoning.	

The article "Should I buy an electric car in 2023?" is intended to help the reader answer the question proposed in the title. The structures, like headings, help to clarify the main points of the article while guiding the reader to gain confidence in EVs as potential cars they might consider driving. The reader learns about cost and battery life, among other aspects of EVs. The chart is easy to understand and just lists a few cars so that a reader doesn't get overwhelmed while still learning about costs, range of driving, and charging times. This information helps the reader to see the feasibility of an EV car. Finally, the most compelling part of the article are the beautiful photos. They are strategically chosen to showcase the glamour and ease of driving an EV. You can stylishly drive down a freeway, park in a garage at the shopping plaza, and charge at a community charging center. All of these scenes are shown to inspire the reader to consider an EV. The article is clear, provides facts to inform the reader and to address common questions, and it shows off attractive cars. Through these structures and with this evidence, the reader might be persuaded to try out an EV in the coming year.

THEIR TURN: PLANNING FOR TEXT FEATURES

Have students practice using the chart in Figure 4.7 to identify purpose, evidence, and structure for a text that relates to an issue they are interested in or studying. To model how to analyze a text for structure, Ms. Hollins uses an article in *Car Magazine*, "Should I buy an electric car in 2023?" (http://bit.ly/3FeD7mX). The text in italics shows ideas around purpose, evidence, and structure. You could use this to model for your students; a blank downloadable version is available at resources.corwin.com/ClassroomToCareer.

It is important to note that features tend to be easier for students to find since they are often obvious, like a map or picture. What Ms. Hollins and Mr. Meyers make sure to emphasize, however, is how to read these elements of a text rather than simply skimming over them, as readers are often wont to do. Each text feature in a model text should be carefully considered, using modeling think-alouds and close readings, and connected to the purpose and readers of the text in question. Ms. Hollins and Mr. Meyer often provide a list of common structures and features for their students (see figure 4.8) to use while they read *and* write to remind them to be on the lookout for these important writing tools.

Figure 4.8 • Common Text Structures and Features

Common text structures	Common text features
Descriptive	Headers
Cause and Effect	Captions
Problem and Solution	Graphics/Illustrations
Sequence/Chronological Order	Labels
Compare/Contrast	Subtitles
	Glossary
	Table of Contents
	Index
	Maps
	Special Print/Font

Text structure, often hinted to by the features, is more subtle and often an accidental result in student writing. Novice writers may create a piece with no plan for the structure only to realize, after it has been written, that it is a problem/solution or a cause/effect structure. Imagine how much more powerful it would be if students knew the structure they were going for *before* they started writing! This is why in the second row of the planner, Ms. Hollins's and Mr. Meyers's students need to identify what specific moves they will make in regard to structure and text features.

"Something I've noticed in my students is that they're somewhat taken aback by the question," Mr. Meyers reveals, "because they've not really considered that part of the writing process for their own work. They see features like images and headers but have never considered them for themselves, because they aren't totally sure how they work at first. Ms. Hollins and I really work at providing multiple exposures to texts that successfully use features and structures we can talk about and unpack as a class."

Once students gain, with the deliberate and direct instruction and modeling of an expert reader—their teacher—an understanding of how the form of a text makes or breaks its function, they can begin to apply these important elements to their own writing, both in and out of the classroom.

SUM IT UP

Just as our real-world example of Tom Erikson demonstrates, the evidence and approach you take toward writing in the workplace very much depends on an understanding of who your audience is, what you want to accomplish in your contact with them, and what details and formats you will use to best accomplish these aims.

For Tom Erikson, understanding of his audience and purpose ensures his patients get the best medical care they can; his writing tasks, if done well, also protect him and his colleagues from misinformation and confusion. Mr. Erikson knows that the evidence he includes in his work, as well as how he presents it, makes an impact on his readers. Our students, too, make an impact in the texts they write for the wide varieties of purposes and audiences they write for; knowing what to include and how to organize it increases their success and efficacy as we prepare them for the outside world. But, as any seasoned writer knows, a first draft is never a final draft if you want to make the biggest impact on your audience. In our next chapter, we will consider the last item on the rubric, *I have used the editing and revision process to refine and tighten my work; there is evidence of change between my first and last drafts.* (Revisit Figure 1.3 for the full rubric.)

ANTICIPATION GUIDE

Revisit the anticipation guide that appeared at the beginning of the chapter to check and expand your initial responses. Even if you had the correct answer, now you can add an explanation that illustrates your deepened understanding.

Possible Fact	True	False
There are three main types of evidence used when writing most texts.	This chapter discusses 6 different types of evidence	X
Rubrics are an effective way to communicate what structures and use of evidence you want your students to use.	X	
Cross-curricular writing projects can encourage real-world application of using evidence and structure for a specific audience.	X	

CHAPTER FIVE

Revision

How Can I Make My Writing Crystal Clear?

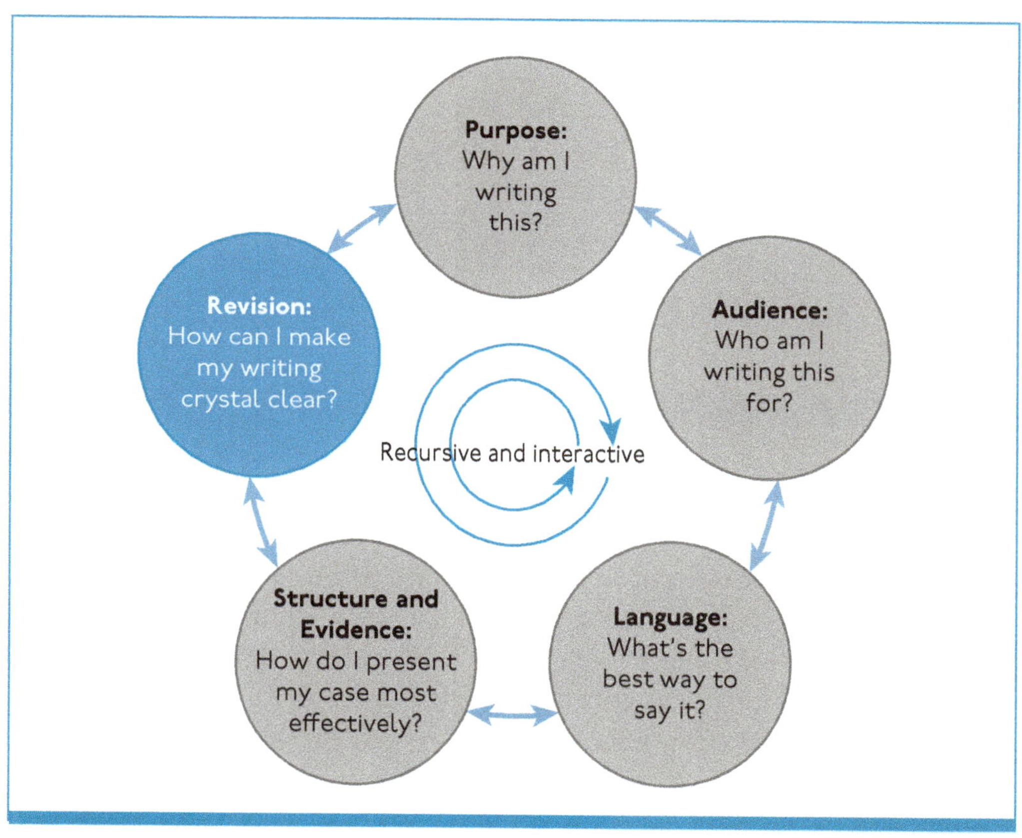

Writing and rewriting are a constant search for what one is saying.

— John Updike

ANTICIPATION GUIDE

This chapter focuses on teaching *revision*. Before you begin reading the chapter, stop for a minute to complete the anticipation guide to check your knowledge of the following information that will be shared throughout the chapter. At the end of the chapter in the *Sum It Up* section, you'll be able to revisit these facts and also self-assess what you've learned.

Use this anticipation guide to assess your beginning understanding:

Anticipation Guide

Possible Fact	True	False
One of the most challenging parts in the revision phase for students is finding the area of their text that needs more work.		
Revision is mostly about punctuation and grammar—making something "publishable."		
Peer feedback isn't effective because most students lack the expertise to help guide each other's writing.		

Most teachers can attest to the importance of the revision process—especially English teachers—in clarifying and refining ideas. The truth is revision *can* and *should* take place in every discipline but can often be seen as an afterthought or a challenging task that can feel difficult to incorporate into classroom norms. This is also true in personal-professional situations. Have you ever been in such a hurry to get a message sent or a paper delivered that you hit the send button, and then when you glanced back, you are aghast with the spelling, grammar, and even content errors you should have revised before sending? Although most recipients of our messages may only grimace at one spelling mistake or one grammatical miscue, they are often more critical about the content of the message. However, once we get to the workplace or begin to prepare applications for workplace situations, many employers do use spelling, grammar, and certainly content as a quasi-measure of capability and definitely as an indicator of one's attention to detail (Place, 2022). Because of this, so many of us are wise enough never to send a response late at night, after a social gathering, or before we take the time to review and revise.

WHAT IS REVISION?

A simple answer to this question is that revision means to take another look or to see (vision) again (re). Revision is not simply about editing the format and punctuation. Instead, when we "do" revision, we are reading a text with the vision of what was intended. From there we can rewrite portions to make the focus clearer and more readily understood. Luckily, it isn't difficult for our students to understand the concept of revision because most use a photo editing program like Retouch, Snapseed, or Photoshop to remove extraneous subjects and objects from their photos. In addition, the revisionist can also alter lighting and people in the photos. If you've ever used a photo app, you know that when you revised your first photo, you probably focused on just one dimension such as lighting. But, as your confidence with using the app grew, you felt more comfortable revising multiple features until you were finally satisfied that you had created a photo that conveyed the meaning you intended to share. The same is true for revising a written text. Many students who write a piece see the text as "one and done," meaning once they're finished with the first draft, they're finished. As Hayes and Flower (1986) note, students often are unable to identify areas in their texts' message that may need revision, nor do they know how to revise once a need for revision is identified. For this reason, it's important for us as teachers to focus on both the value and process of revision, which includes replacing ideas and language, adding new information, deleting repeated ideas and details, and reordering the flow of ideas (Anderson & Gallagher, 2012) until the message intended is truly deemed as shared. Unlike editing, which makes changes to sentence structuring, and phrasing, revision involves making substantial changes to sequence, ideas, voice, language, and argument. Both processes change the document, but revising does so in a much more substantial way.

Strengthening writing through multiple drafts requires feedback that both zooms in while still assessing the work holistically. Both types of feedback may happen simultaneously, or a writer may choose to focus on garnering one type depending on their needs. To see this in practice, consider high school senior Simon Bishop, who is looking forward to finishing up his final writing assignment for an online college poetry course. This essay proved to be more challenging for Simon, even though he's a strong writer, and he relied on the expertise of his peers to help him refine his thinking.

"I ask for help when I hit an obstacle; when I am done with something, I like to get another opinion to make sure it is on the right track; sometimes I'll want someone to look at the whole thing, but for this essay I needed help making sure I sounded consistent," Simon notes. "This was a really long paper, so I couldn't finish it all in one sitting; I needed help making sure my ideas worked together."

Simon knows he isn't finished writing just because a draft is completed. What Simon also knows, but maybe not consciously, is that there are different ways to approach revision. Instead of wanting feedback on the entire piece (global revision/feedback), Simon wanted specific feedback on his wording and consistency (local revision/feedback). For a different type of paper, say a data-heavy analysis argument, an accuracy check might be more appropriate. Much like the drafting process, the revision process is varied and highly dependent on the task, reader, and writer. Explore Figure 5.1 to gain a better understanding of the different types of revision.

Figure 5.1 • Approaches to Revision

Global vs. Local	Global revision requires a holistic view of the piece and considers its impact as a finished artifact. Here is where you may consider things like purpose, audience, and message. Local revision calls attention to a specific area of the paper (see the following sections for areas that might be considered in a local revision).
Accuracy	Is the information correct? Akin to proofreading, this type of revision is best done by a knowledgeable reader who can assess the validity of the information and formatting/citation methods.
Proofreading	Does the writing adhere to an established Style Guide or template? Does the writing follow established writing conventions and grammar rules?
Structure	How does the form of the work interact with and enhance its message? Is the organization logical? Does it follow the structure of texts within its genre? Are there areas of weakness that need to be developed to further the message (perhaps, for example, an area where the writer might clarify or elaborate on their thinking)?
Style	What is the tone of the piece? Is it appropriate to the audience and conventions of the genre it is written in? If appropriate, is there a unique and consistent authorial voice?

As Simon noted, he doesn't ask for help on *everything* in his paper but rather knows the areas he wants more advice on. Simon explains, "In sixth grade we had steps for submitting a piece of work—our teacher wouldn't just accept the first thing we wrote. She would give us example essays for errors [and] modeled how to revise them—then we'd practice and then apply it to our own work. It was a full system: planning—Rough Draft—Peer Review—Final draft, and I still use it today!" To ensure more students think like Simon, we want to make sure we create the opportunities where our students have a chance to see models of expert thinking around revision (like teacher Shelby Brown's think-aloud, which comes later in the chapter) and then implement those skills with their own writing.

WHY SHOULD WE FOCUS ON UNDERSTANDING REVISION?

Statistics teacher Shelby Brown is confronting this very question in her students' written analyses of data on an assignment where they were asked to consider and share their positions about the original authorship of Beyoncé songs. "I had students examine the Beyoncé song 'Crazy in Love' and track the average word length. Students then used these data to compare with songs that are verified as Beyoncé-written. They had just turned in their written claims about the data and I saw they were having trouble with the reasoning behind the claims; they were using all of the terminology we covered in class, but I could tell they didn't deeply understand the material, as they hadn't taken time to return to the sources to validate the information they shared. In many instances they were so sure of their positions that it was obvious they hadn't reviewed their statements to validate content or check sources or even their spelling and grammar." Typically students in Ms. Brown's class would turn this assignment in and they either "got it" or they didn't; however, because Ms. Brown asked them to share this information in a final draft that could be extended to a larger audience than the class, she was focusing on revision Ms. Brown explained it this way: "I really want to show them how to use revision to make their interpretations and presentations of the data better and geared toward a specific audience—but how?"

Ms. Brown's students, like many of our students, are using writing to express their thinking, but—as Updike pointed out in the opening quote—they may still be searching for what they want to *say*. The revision process (which includes sharing work with peers and other adults) is our students' chance to use teacher-made or personal success criteria as a way to assess progress toward a writing objective, and it is an opportunity to "test out" writing on a real-life audience. From there, students can take the feedback received and refine their work to make it more relevant and effective. Because revision is an integral part of the writing process, it is the final criterion in the rubric that Ms. Brown used to support her students' writing efforts (figure 5.2). Note the last criterion: *I have used the revision processes to refine and tighten my work; there is evidence of change between my first and last drafts.*

Figure 5.2 ◆ Revision Process Writing Rubric

Needs Work	Meets Expectations	Exceeds Expectations
	My writing has a **clear, locatable purpose and message.** I have **demonstrated knowledge of my audience by:** • **My word choice** (I have used language that is appropriate to my audience). • **My use of evidence** (I have included examples, illustrations, and other artifacts that will best convince my audience). • **My tone** (I have made certain stylistic choices to further my purpose with my audience). • **My formatting choices** (I have considered the structure and associated features that best suit my purpose and audience). I have **used outside, credible sources to support my thinking.** I have **used the revision process to refine and tighten my work;** there is evidence of change between my first and last drafts. I have **solicited feedback** from a non-classmate and included a feedback form.	

YOUR TURN: DRAFT WRITING AND RUBRIC TO MODELS

Provide your students with short, sustained writing experiences that focus on the revision process. See the prompt below, which Tanya Wright's science class is using to practice persuasive letter writing. Try this out yourself first, so that you will have a model to show to students:

"Write a short, rough-draft response to this scenario and prompt: The administration and school board are deciding how to spend a large donation given by an anonymous donor to the school. The donor stipulated that the funds must be spent on equipment and materials for students. You have suggestions that would help guide the decision around what to purchase with this donation. Your task is to write a proposal to the administrators and board members outlining your ideas. Because this is a rough draft and you will have an opportunity for future revision, you are given a time limit of five minutes for your first iteration of this letter. Set your timer and start writing."

After you've written your first draft, use the rubric from Figure 5.2 to determine areas for revision. Now, rewrite your proposal given your thinking around revision. Consider sharing with students this example of draft-writing, thinking through needed revision using a rubric, and rewriting with "needs work" ideas in mind. You can think aloud to showcase your cognitive processes as you model. Figure 5.2a shows "needs work" ideas in italics, composed by a science teacher reflecting on her letter request for science equipment.

Figure 5.2a ◆ Writing Rubric—Teacher Example

Needs Work	Meets Expectations	Exceeds Expectations
My message could be clearer; I need to explain how money spent for better lab equipment will enhance the science program. Perhaps I should list the courses that need new equipment and explain how students will use it. That will be more compelling.	My writing has a **clear, locatable purpose and message.** I have **demonstrated knowledge of my audience by:** • **My word choice** (I have used language that is appropriate to my audience).	

(Continued)

(Continued)

Needs Work	Meets Expectations	Exceeds Expectations
I've used some technical science language, like "titration," and I'm not sure my audience will understand this. I should clarify more. *My tone is a bit abrupt and demanding. ("You must provide new equipment for science teachers.") I'll try to sound friendlier but still professional.* *I need to add my contact information, the date, and note that I am a teacher in the science department. I was also the chair of the department for three years. I can revise the formatting to include this in my signature.* *I'll revise this!*	• **My use of evidence** (I have included examples, illustrations, and other artifacts that will best convince my audience). • **My tone** (I have made certain stylistic choices to further my purpose with my audience). • **My formatting choices** (I have considered the structure and associated features that best suit my purpose and audience). I have **used outside, credible sources** to support my thinking. I have **used the revision process to refine and tighten my work**; there is evidence of change between my first and last drafts. I have **solicited feedback** from a non-classmate and included a feedback form.	

THEIR TURN: REVISING WRITING USING A RUBRIC

To help students practice, consider a local or global issue that students can study and then write about using their informed, reflective writing voice. Here's an example from another science class to consider:

The issue of where to construct power plants is rooted in controversy, primarily due to the harmful emissions that are a by-product of fossil fuel energy production. Ask students to review this EPA web page: http://bit.ly/3Tle4nY.

After his students have reviewed the information on the page, Bruce Thrace, a life science teacher, has his students look at the interactive map that breaks down information around power plant location, fuel produced, and neighborhood demographics (income, percent people of color, and education level). Then, he provides the following task:

"Write a script for a speech that will be presented to a community board expressing your opinion on a fictional proposal for the construction of a neighborhood power plant somewhere within a one hundred-mile radius of your neighborhood. You have thirty minutes to review data and write your first draft. You'll be able to review, edit, and revise."

Next, he tells his students, "After you've finished your draft writing, revisit your first draft using a rubric. After you've considered what needs work and what exceeds expectations, go back to your writing and make appropriate edits and revisions." (See Figure 5.2b, which shows an example of a student's revision work in Mr. Thrace's class.)

Figure 5.2b • Writing Rubric – Student Example

Needs Work	Meets Expectations	Exceeds Expectations
Move the purpose to the beginning. I think I should explain the term "environmental justice." I'm going to look this up, so that I define it for the readers and so that I can connect it to my purpose. I should clarify the data a little more and explain why it's important to my purpose. I could talk more about who lives in the neighborhoods where power plants are located since I have the demographic data from the map resource. I still need to reference my sources. I remember that my teacher said that it's important to cite my sources. I also want to reread again to be sure	My writing has a **clear, locatable purpose and message.** I have **demonstrated knowledge of my audience by:** • **My word choice** (I have used language that is appropriate to my audience). • **My use of evidence** (I have included examples, illustrations, and other artifacts that will best convince my audience). • **My tone** (I have made certain stylistic choices to further my purpose with my audience). • **My formatting choices** (I have considered the structure and associated features that best suit my purpose and audience).	My purpose is clear, but I think I could move it to the beginning of my writing, so that it's what the readers see first. I am using data from the data map! My tone is serious since this is an important issue. I think that is appropriate.

(Continued)

(Continued)

Needs Work	Meets Expectations	Exceeds Expectations
I have all my grammar correct. *I need to go back in and make the changes I mentioned.*	I have **used outside, credible sources to support my thinking.** I have **used the revision process to refine and tighten my work;** there is evidence of change between my first and last drafts. I have **solicited feedback** from a non-classmate and included a feedback form.	

HOW DO WE SUPPORT STUDENTS TO REVISE THEIR WRITING?

Peer revision is often a necessary skill to have once you enter the workplace and appears hand in hand with collaborative projects. Becka Menke uses peer revision and success criteria daily in her position as a senior city planner. In her position, Ms. Menke notes that revision takes place in all levels of her job: "The city has a formal review process for all external documents. So my supervisor, the city attorney, and the deputy director, all evaluate documents according to our style guide, or for specific sections we are looking for." For Ms. Menke and her colleagues, it is imperative to be familiar with how to revise but also what to do next.

Knowledge of formal revision processes are important, of course, but Becka also points out that "much of my feedback for my colleagues is actually centered around who the document is going to. Depending on who might be reading it, I offer different advice to my peers about how to revise and edit their writing." Ms. Menke has a strong sense of who the audience of her and her peers' writing is, and this drives the type of feedback she gives, in addition to making sure she adheres to guidelines set by the city style guide. "I also always check the type of document I am editing and make sure it is serving the purpose it was supposed to fulfill," Becka notes. In her case, audience and purpose are the driving forces behind the suggestions she recommends to her peers, even though she may not have a formal revision process at work.

PAUSE AND CONSIDER

What types of activities can you include in your classroom to promote metacognition during the revision stage of writing? Where are opportunities for students to self-assess and set goals in your class? What about chances for peer-to-peer feedback? Look back through chapters 1 through 4 and think about how you might include self-assessment and revision in each phase of the writing process.

____

____

____

____

____

To connect the revision process in the work world back to the instruction we do in the classroom, let's return to Sylvia Brown's statistics class for a moment. Like Ms. Menke, Ms. Sylvia Brown, the statistics teacher, knows her students will need to be able to give and receive feedback on their writing throughout school and in their careers. She wonders, "How can I give my students authentic opportunities to give clear and actionable feedback to their peers, receive this feedback, and make effective and meaningful revisions to their work?"

Modeling Audience and Purpose

"Explain your findings and reasoning like you would to Belinda, my mom, who knows little to nothing about statistics. The measure of knowledge is often the ability to teach others about what you know."

Ms. Brown is changing her approach to the statistical analysis of song lyrics to remind her students of audience and purpose in their writing. She revisits the original prompt for her students: "Based on the evidence collected, is Beyoncé the author of the song 'Crazy in Love'? Be sure to use evidence *and* reasoning to explain your answer to someone not in our class." She reminds them that their audience is someone who may need extra explanation in order to understand the analysis, "Remember," she says, "Belinda is the type of audience we're writing to, so we have to make sure to connect the dots for her."

To model how students might use claims, evidence, and reasoning, Ms. Brown uses a think-aloud to demonstrate the moves a writer takes when revising their work. "I know that my purpose is to explain whether or not, using the evidence collected, Beyoncé writes her own songs, so when I look at my writing and want to revise it, I want to make sure I've answered this question." She goes on, "I *also* know, as a statistician, that it is essential to be able to communicate what I find through my work to others, especially those who may not be familiar with statistics. Therefore, I need to make sure I am translating the math I do for a wider audience by clearly explaining what my data is *and* what it means."

To connect the current learning to prior instructions and other classes she reminds them "this response is going to fit the Claim-Evidence-Reasoning (CER) structure I use in all of my classes, so I'll want to make sure I have all three parts when I am finished. I'm already noting that I do make a claim—I say that we don't have enough evidence to prove Beyoncé wrote 'Crazy in Love'—and I have evidence, too. I say that her average word length per sentence in songs she has verified authorship on is 3.64 and that the average word length in 'Crazy in Love' is 3.53." Ms. Brown knows that a well-crafted think-aloud is crucial in helping to model the revision process for her students.

Creating Models Using Error Analysis

The model text Ms. Brown is using in her think-aloud reflects the common errors she sees in her classes' responses. The process of identifying student errors by reviewing student work is called error analysis. After errors have been identified, the teacher should next provide strategic scaffolds and engage in targeted reteaching. To complete the process of error analysis, Ms. Brown reviews her classes' work holistically using her rubric (or criteria) and looks for patterns and common errors students make in order to target her reteaching (Marzano, 2009). She will note which students need reteaching in which aspects of the rubric or criteria she is using, writing their initials in the category they need more practice in. Using this method, she may reteach small groups of students, or if everyone struggles with a certain concept, extend a lesson for the whole class. See Figure 5.3 to see how Ms. Brown tracks common errors in her students' work.

Figure 5.3 • CER Paragraph Error Analysis

Period	Making clear claims	Using appropriate evidence	Connecting evidence to claim with reasoning
1	E.J. L.J M.T. S.T.	E.J. T.R. Y.M. L.I. L.L.	E.J. Y.M. L.I.
2	Z.K A.B.	N.M. P. M. C.M. S.A.	M.M. A.B.
3	S.R. J.L. H.P. B.H. A.H.	B.H. A.H.	B.H. A.H.
4	S.J. M.S. D.S. M.P.	S.J. M.S. B.M.	B.M. M.M. S.F.

She continues, "I know that sometimes, especially in math, I feel like the evidence speaks for itself, so I forget to include reasoning, which is exactly what my audience needs, since they weren't in the class to see how we calculated everything. I have to remember that my audience is Belinda, who isn't a statistician, so I have to connect the dots for her. That means I am going to need to say something after I state my evidence to show her why I came to that conclusion. For example, I might say "because a writer's word length is typically consistent, I would look for a number close to 3.64 to confirm Beyoncé's authorship on any unverified songs; since 3.53 is very close, we can safely assume that she authored 'Crazy in Love' as well, if we are using sentence length to establish authorship. I might also include any figures or visuals that helped me come to my conclusion."

Before she wraps up, Ms. Brown models the final step of using success criteria to recheck revised work: "Now, let me go back and see if I can make sure I have all three parts of the C-E-R format." Ms. Brown underlines her claim, circles her evidence, and boxes her reasoning, a method her students use. She has modeled for her students how to consistently keep audience and purpose in mind to help revise their writing in Math. See Figure 5.4 for an example of work from Ms. Brown's student.

Figure 5.4 • Activity From StatsMedic.com

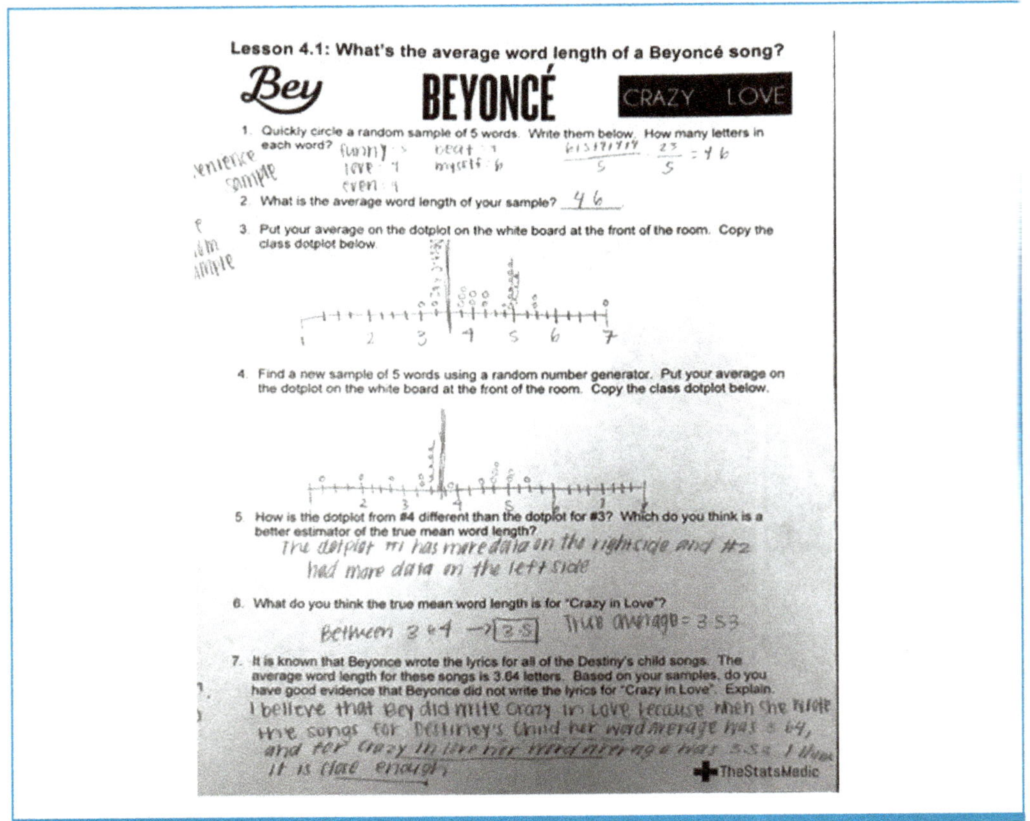

PAUSE AND CONSIDER

Jot down a few ways you might use error analysis to tailor your instruction to your students' need in the revision phase of writing. Think about Chapters 1–4; how might error analysis come into play during the different parts of the writing process?

____

____

____

____

____

____

YOUR TURN: TEACHER PRACTICE
DESIGN A REVISION THINK-ALOUD

Consider this text, written by Daniel, who takes his grandmother for strolls in her wheelchair several times a week. He's found that the design of the wheelchair could be improved and has written an email to the manufacturer with his suggestions:

To Whom It May Concern,

I'm writing to let you know of a problem. I am suggesting that you develop a new model of a wheelchair that has push handles that can be raised and lowered. The wheelchair my grandmother has doesn't work this way and it's a problem. I hope that you will take this advice and build a better wheelchair. Sincerely- Daniel

Just like any other skill, you can model for revision for students by thinking aloud. Show students how you would revise Daniel's writing using a think-aloud focused on audience and purpose. The example in Figure 5.5 shows one way to model. Try to create your own think-aloud.

Figure 5.5 • Modeling a Revision Think-Aloud

Example	Revised Writing
Name the strategy, skill, or task. "Today I am going to show you . . ." how to think about audience and purpose when you are rereading and revising your writing.	
State the purpose of the strategy, skill, or task. "Because writers need to clarify . . ." their purpose for writing, I'm going to add more details about my idea for push handles that can be raised or lowered.	*Because I am a tall person—six foot two inches—it's difficult for me to reach when the push handles are in a low fixed position. Having movable handles would make pushing more comfortable for me. If a shorter person pushes the wheelchair, they would appreciate being able to lower the handles.*
Explain when the strategy or skill is used. "When I'm done with my first draft, I usually . . ." reread a few times to be sure that I don't have any grammar or style mistakes, such as having my closure and signature on the same line. I'll fix that and I'll leave a space for my actual signature.	*Sincerely yours,* *Daniel Jones* *Daniel Jones*

(Continued)

(Continued)

Example	Revised Writing
Use analogies to link prior knowledge to new learning. "I know that readers need . . . , therefore I'm going to . . . " *Readers need examples and clarity . . . so I'm going to revise my final sentences to be more specific about my suggestions for a new model.*	*The wheelchair my grandmother has doesn't have movable push handles which makes it more challenging for me to push. I have to stoop down. I'm sure that many of your customers would be happy to acquire a new wheelchair if you included a feature that would make it easier to push friends and family members in wheelchairs.*
Demonstrate how the skill, strategy, or task is completed. "I'm going to show . . ." *how I revise my closing lines so that they are friendlier but still formal.*	*Thank you for considering my idea. I hope to hear from you. I'd also appreciate learning about any new features you are currently implementing in your newer models.*
Alert learners to errors to avoid. "I'm going to watch for . . . " *redundancy, so I will check to see if I'm repeating any words or phrases or ideas. I see that I said "problem" twice, so I'll revise the first sentence.*	*I'm writing to let you know of a concern I have and an idea that might help.*
Assess the use of the skill. Now I'm going to . . . *reread the whole revised letter.*	*To Whom It May Concern,* *I'm writing to let you know of a concern I have and an idea that might help. I am suggesting that you develop a new model of a wheelchair that has push handles that can be raised and lowered. The wheelchair my grandmother has doesn't have moveable push handles, which makes it more challenging for me to push. I have to stoop down. I'm sure that many of your customers would be happy to acquire a new wheelchair if you included a feature that would make it easier to push friends and family members in wheelchairs.* *Thank you for considering my idea. I hope to hear from you. I'd also appreciate learning about any new features you are currently implementing in your newer models.* *Sincerely yours,* *Daniel Jones*

Adapted from Fisher et al., 2010.

Peer Feedback: Leveraging Student Knowledge to Develop Writing and Career Skills

To help her students continue to guide their revision efforts, Ms. Brown created a feedback form for students to fill out before they solicit feedback from an outside reader (see Figure 5.6). Ms. Brown created this general feedback form for her students in collaboration with her grade-level English teacher, Mr. Herold. Notice that the feedback form requires the writer to identify an audience and purpose. The intent is to prompt student writers to keep audience and purpose in mind when writing and revising. Knowing who you are communicating with changes how you say what you say and the types of evidence you include to prove your thinking. Reaffirming who the audience is throughout the revision process can help highlight areas where a writer can more effectively reach their audience. The last section of the feedback form provides an opportunity to do just that.

Figure 5.6 • Peer Feedback Form

Writer Name: ______________________________

Reviewer Name: ______________________________

<table>
<tr><td>Writer fill out this section</td></tr>
<tr><td>Purpose for writing (what do you want the reader to think or believe?):

You want the reader to know you have a suggestion for a wheelchair modification.

Who is your audience?

You are writing to someone who you think can help make that change happen. It's addressed to Whom It May Concern. Maybe you should see if you can find the name of a representative of the company, so you can be sure that someone actually reads this note.</td></tr>
<tr><td>Reviewer fill out this section</td></tr>
<tr><td>Did the author achieve their purpose?

Yes, the author makes the problem clear and provides a solution to the issue of wheelchair handles.

How? Where?

The author of the note suggests movable handles. The author also shares a bit about personal experience, which makes the writing more compelling and realistic.

What revisions do they need to make to strengthen their purpose?

The personal experience part (the author pushing his grandma in a wheelchair and struggling with handles that are too low) could be expanded to illustrate the problem. Overall, it's a strong letter. Perhaps the author could request a response more directly—"I'd like to hear back from you to find out if you like this idea and if it would be possible to implement it."</td></tr>
</table>

(Continued)

(Continued)

> **What are three consistent errors you observed in their writing?**
>
> *The author should use a letter format with the signature on a separate line.*
>
> *The author should include more details.*
>
> *I only see two errors.*
>
> **How can they better reach their intended audience?**
>
> *Add more details about the problem. The author could also talk to other users of wheelchairs to see if they have similar issues with the height of handles. Having more data to substantiate the problem would be compelling.*

THEIR TURN: PRACTICE PEER FEEDBACK

Consider an activity like the following one from Tabitha Goodwin's Art History course.

Select a work of art from the Smithsonian American Art Museum web page: https://americanexperience.si.edu/historical-eras/contemporary-united-states/

Ask students to read about a work of art to explore the cultural and historical significance. They will then write a paragraph that could appear in the signage for the art piece, explaining context and other related aspects students have learned about. After they write, each student will complete the top part—the writer part—of the Peer Feedback Form. Then students will share their writing with a peer, and reviewer will fill in the bottom section of the Peer Feedback Form.

Students can practice using their peer's feedback to revise their writing. The example in Figure 5.5a demonstrates how to describe purpose and audience.

Just as most writing partners regularly collaborate on writing, our students would be well-served to learn how to effectively use the peer revision process. There is a wealth of evidence reinforcing that peer support in the writing process boosts growth in multiple areas. According to a study conducted in 3rd through 12th grade classrooms, students who participated in self-grading and peer-grading performed better on tests than those who did not. This study also found that student and teacher grades were the same, with the average of students rating themselves and their peers similarly to their teachers (Sanchez et al., 2017). Armed with this knowledge, 12th grade English Teacher Carmen Harrington created what she calls "The Writing Lab":

I was inspired by the university writing lab we had on campus when I was in college; it was open to all majors and staffed by trained student tutors. It was free to registered students, and the only requirement was that you had to come in with an idea of what you wanted help with." As you can probably guess, Ms. Harrington was stymied by the fact that she didn't know what she didn't know. "I was stuck," she says, "I had never been asked to identify what I needed help with before. In high school peer review days were sort of perfunctory, mind-numbing worksheets you had to fill out. I don't think I ever actually learned how to help myself or anyone else!

Like Ms. Harrington, many students aren't given practice and opportunities to ask themselves, "what do I really need help with?" As mentioned above, self-grading and peer-grading can have significant effects on student progress, not to mention that those two skills are ever present in the workplace. Ms. Harrington's "writing lab" requires students to use a reflection sheet that prompts them to provide information on their writing and identify the type of help they anticipate they will need. This metacognitive process pushes students to not only use the prompts and rubrics provided to them by their teachers but encourages self-reflection and efficacy as they figure out what they know, where they are at in the writing process, and where they need to go next (see Figure 5.6; a blank downloadable version is available at resources.corwin.com/ClassroomToCareer).

Figure 5.6a • Peer Feedback Form Example

Writer fill out this section
Purpose for writing (what do you want the reader to think or believe?):
I wanted to convey my understanding of Kerry James Marshall's painting called SOB, SOB, which was painted in 2003. Marshall paints pictures about African American history and culture. I want to explain that the girl is crying about the book she is reading called "Africa since 1413."
Who is your audience?
My audience is people who like art, but may not be art history experts, so I need to be clear, have explanations, and explain any academic terms.

Reviewer fill out this section
Did the author achieve their purpose?

(Continued)

(Continued)

How? Where?

What revisions do they need to make to strengthen their purpose?

What are three consistent errors you observed in their writing?

How can they better reach their intended audience?

Figure 5.7 • Writing Lab Form

Writer Name: Sharla Brown	

Prompt and Audience (What question/prompt are you answering? Who is it for?)

I'm addressing this prompt: Write to the director of the hospital you work at, requesting that your nursing team be provided with a budget to update the supplies and materials in your "department needs" to be able to care for patients.

What type of revision help do you need (circle one)?

Planning	Global	Local	Accuracy	Structure	(Style)

What, specifically, do you need help with?

I'd like feedback on the tone of my note. I want to be professional and clear. I also want my request to sound compelling and important. Since I'm writing to my boss, I want to be respectful, too.

Tutor notes:

Let's work on being concise, using clear language, and providing evidence to support requests.

Tutor signature/stamp:

After filling out the sheet, students are paired with a trained peer tutor who will assist them in revising their work (you'll notice "proofreading/editing" is absent from the list, as the lab is more geared towards student-centered changes rather than a tutor "fixing" mistakes). After the session, the tutor makes notes on what was worked on and stamps the sheet using a stamp unique to them. This allows Ms. Harrington to check in on progress with the tutor who helped the student, as well as offer feedback to the tutor themselves. "What I've noticed most," Carmen mentions, "is that students rely so much less on me now once they've begun writing. It's like the lab gave them permission to be in charge of their and their peer's work. I've never seen them more successful."

While Carmen Harrington's "writing lab" may not be a possibility for your site or schedule, prioritizing time for students to reflect on theirs' and others' work *meaningfully and intentionally* provides numerous benefits, both now and in the future. Whether it be improved motivation and performance on assessments, or increased confidence and competence in the writing process, placing power in the hands of student writers will give them the opportunity to learn and practice skills that will be with them for a lifetime.

SUM IT UP

Although we may be tempted to upload a proposal that has been lingering a bit too long on our to-do list or hit "send" on an email we have been crafting for a few days, it is important to remember that, in many instances, our first drafts shouldn't be our *last* drafts—and the same holds true for our students. While it can often feel like the most expendable part of the writing process, the revision phase is a crucial part of making sure our writing achieves the purpose we have carefully planned for through close attention to our audience and their needs. Thoughtful and thorough revision helps us (and our students) to reflect on our writing via self-assessment or peer feedback which quite literally offers an opportunity to see our writing through another's eyes. By identifying what the tools are needed to self-assess writing, like rubrics and success criteria, we can teach students how to use them to locate areas for feedback and take the appropriate next steps. Apprenticing our students into the feedback and revision cycle through modeling and targeted instruction like Ms. Brown will enable them to become better writers, of course, but will also lay the foundation for purposeful and fruitful collaboration with others, as evidenced by Becka Menke's workplace experiences. Once our students see the value in using peers to revise their work, they will be empowered with yet another tool that will enable them to create powerful, meaningful, and purposeful texts that truly accomplish what the writer intended.

ANTICIPATION GUIDE

Revisit the anticipation guide that appeared at the beginning of the chapter to check and expand your initial responses. Even if you had the correct answer, now you can add an explanation that illustrates your deepened understanding.

Possible Fact	True	False	Explanation
One of the most challenging parts in the revision phase for students is finding the area of their text that needs more work.	X		
Revision is mostly about punctuation and grammar-making something "publishable."		X	Revision centers on replacing ideas and language, adding new information, deleting repeated ideas and details, and reordering the flow of ideas.
Peer feedback isn't effective since most students lack the grammatical expertise to help guide each other's writing.		X	Peer reviewers can provide multiple levels of feedback that don't include grammar and punctuation, including ideas, language, organization, and use of details.

CHAPTER SIX

Putting It All Together
Writing Readiness Equals Career Readiness

We've shared many reasons people write in workplace situations and also ideas to help you get your students ready for every writing task they will be called to complete after they leave high school. Toward the goal of supporting students to learn how to competently write in all situations, we've looked at models of the types of writing they'll be asked to compose in their daily work lives. The models will vary depending on the types of careers they choose or the situational goals they must accomplish. Most adults are called on to write at some time in their workplace situation or write to convey an idea or intent to a specified audience in their communities. What differs is the writing expectations of each career or situation.

Regardless of a person's assigned or chosen writing task, the point we've emphasized throughout each chapter is that a writer can succeed if they **identify models** that are similar to the one they are attempting to write and then pay close attention to how the author of the model used language and tone to purposefully craft a text to convey a message to the particular audience. To bring it all together, let's investigate the three considerations when crafting a work text: identify models, examine models in a structured way, and read widely and apply analysis skills.

Figure 6.1 • Considerations When Crafting a Work Text

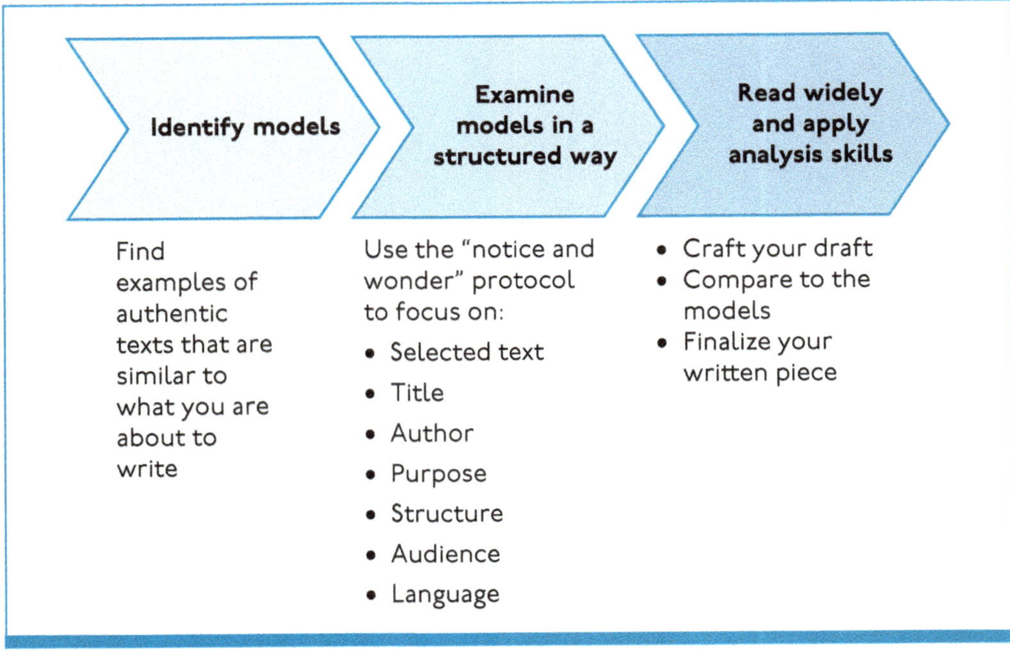

PAUSE AND CONSIDER

How do you currently use model texts in your classroom? How can you leverage your knowledge of your students to find meaningful writing models to study? What do you need to know about your students? Where might you find these models?

IDENTIFY MODELS OF THE INTENDED TEXTS

In every workplace, employees are asked to write some type of text either for themselves as a series of notes or to share with an identified audience. Additionally, as we've noted throughout the chapters of this text, even when not requested, employees also see the need to share their ideas via some form of a written text, be it verbally in person or on the phone, or in a written communique. Details about the format, language, tone, and examples of the message to be crafted depend on the audience receiving the message and the purpose of the message. Because each profession uses specific terms and assumes certain bases of knowledge on the part of the participants, it's important when communicating ideas to "be on the same page" as others in the specific work or professional community. Therefore, it's important to understand the subtleties of communication within the workplace or professional situation whether your ideas are about to be shared via memos, business letters, progress reports, newsletters, data tables, notes, texts, and so forth.

That's why throughout this book we've advocated for you, our educator colleagues, to promote and encourage students to examine models before sharing either written or spoken communications in a professional setting. The language, tone, and level of familiarity conveyed in each model should be analyzed to identify a match between the intent and the message about to be shared.

Many models can be found or created by searching the Internet or by using artificial intelligence text generators. We encourage you to teach your students to use each of these as resources, as models to guide the crafting of their own written texts. Figure 6.2 provides an example of a text requested of ChatGPT that we would share with students. Once shared, together we would analyze it to identify audience, voice, tone, and style. With this knowledge we would work with our students to practice using the model text to craft their own text. In addition to analyzing the features of the model, we would reinforce that these models **are resources** to guide, not to copy or to claim as one's own. This is a perfect way to emphasize the responsibility to avoid plagiarism when analyzing a model. Of course, when using any Internet resource, it's essential to verify that it is safe and secure in terms of user data and personal information.

Dear [Client Name],

I am writing to inform you that we will be turning off all the water supply to your property in order to carry out some necessary plumbing work from 7:00 a.m. until 6:00 p.m. on Friday. This will unfortunately mean that you will not have access to any water during this time.

We understand that this may cause some inconvenience and we apologize for any disruption this may cause. Our team will work as quickly as possible to complete the required work and restore the water supply to your property as soon as possible.

Please ensure that you have enough water stored for the duration of the work and avoid using any appliances or fixtures that require water until the supply is restored. We will keep you informed of any updates throughout the process.

Thank you for your understanding and cooperation. If you have any questions or concerns, please do not hesitate to contact us.

Best regards,
[Plumber's Name]

THEIR TURN: ANALYZE MODEL AND WRITE YOUR OWN

Together with students analyze this model text for tone, voice, language. Is all information given? What's missing? Once analyzed, work with them to use this model to craft their own.

Tone: Direct, professional

Voice: Very approachable but factual

Intent: Share problem

Student's rewrite:

Good morning, Just sharing a heads-up that we'll be turning off your water supply for three hours tomorrow. This inconvenience will occur between 10a.m.–1p.m. There's a leak in your main water pipe so we cannot avoid doing this. I apologize for this and will work with speed to make these repairs.

Please let me know if you have any questions and please know how much I appreciate your understanding.

Pat, Your plumber

EXAMINE MODELS IN A STRUCTURED WAY

To help students pay attention to the nuances of a particular writing example that either you or they have selected, use the "notice-and-wonder" protocol (Figure 6.3; a downloadable version is available from the online companion, resources.corwin.com/WritingClassroomCareer). Begin by explaining the "notice-and-wonder" protocol organizer to students and discussing why and how the information in this organizer could support their writing. Introduce the components of the organizer, which should be familiar to many students.

Figure 6.3 • Notice-and-Wonder Graphic Organizer

Title of Article, Author, and Where to Find It	
Purpose Identify the reason the author is writing this piece. What is the intent?	
Structure identifies the ways in which the author constructs the text **Were these techniques used?** • flashbacks or flash forwards • literary montage (a few pictures or scenes to tell the story) • vignettes • journaling • chronology If used, were they effective?	I notice . . . I wonder . . .
Audience Who is this piece intended for?	I notice . . . I wonder . . .
Language What style of language did the writer use? Notice the words, notice the jargon, and notice the abbreviations	I notice . . . I wonder . . .

Note that the protocol allows for analyzing a text in a structured, organized way. Clarify that students should individually write notes identifying what they notice about the featured text. These "noticings" may be related to the structure of the text, writing techniques, and the type of language used by the author. After students have identified the more obvious aspects of the text, they can begin to analyze it further by positing "wonderings" about the text or about the author. This leads to discussions about purpose, audience, and author's craft.

The notice-and-wonder protocol helps to guide students in seeing how aspects of a written piece reveal the purpose of the writer. Invite students to pay attention to structure (letter format, casual language, etc.) and to use of language (flashbacks or flash forwards, literary montage, such as a few pictures or scenes to tell the story, vignettes, journaling, chronology).

Next, help students to see the use of the protocol in action by modeling what you **notice and wonder** when looking at a focus text. Encourage students to observe what you are noticing and wondering about in a selected focus text and to also consider what information the writer could have included that would have made the intent or purpose of this text more obvious.

Figure 6.4 provides an example of a teacher modeling for a class how to use the "notice-and-wonder" organizer while reading a restaurant review and documenting it. Every noticing and wondering connects to discovering the author's purpose in this instance.

Following is the teacher think-aloud that accompanied the creation of the example organizer in Figure 6.4:

> Well, I found this article in the "Tin Fork" section of this week's *Reader*; since I'm an aspiring food critic, I am interested in this type of writing and want to know how to replicate it. I notice this piece is in the "Restaurants" section of this paper along with other reviews, so I wonder what makes it different. Let me write these things down, though, before I forget. I also notice the author writes in first person, which I know could go in the "Structure" section, but since I am establishing purpose right now, I have a feeling this is important. I'll write it down. Notice the title—"I've gone crazy and ordered a breakfast salad"— that is really unconventional! I am wondering if this writer's purpose is to not only evaluate and judge but also express and reflect since the writer's style is so unique.

The notice-and-wonder protocol draws students' attention to what they see in the text in order to be able to come to some conclusions about it and to facilitate their application of this knowledge to their own writing. Be sure to model your thinking first; then, let students try it out.

Figure 6.4 • Notice-and-Wonder Graphic Organizer.

Article title and author	"I've gone crazy and ordered a breakfast salad," by Ed Bedford, https://www.sandiegoreader.com/news/2018/dec/13/tin-fork-ive-gone-crazy-ordered-breakfast-salad/.
Purpose Identify the reason the author is writing this piece. What is the intent?	I notice . . . this is near other reviews in the "restaurants" section of the paper. This is written in first person using casual language. The title—not expected. I wonder . . . if this is somehow different from the other reviews. Is the tone meant to appeal to "everyday" people? This is meant to entertain, too?
Structure identifies the ways in which the author constructs the text. Were these techniques used? • flashbacks or flash forwards • literary montage (a few pictures or scenes to tell the story) • vignettes • journaling • chronology • cause and effect • other structures If used, were they effective?	I notice . . . this article is a newspaper with lots of photos that describe the food in the article. I wonder . . . if the author is trying to seem like a friend giving the reader a tip about good food.
Audience Who is this piece intended for?	I notice . . . that the author sounds like he's writing to the public- anyone who wants to read this. It's very friendly. I wonder . . . why he uses first person? Here's an example: "Truth is, I'm desperate for brekky. And also, I wanna try this place I've heard about. Has a, uh, breakfast salad."
Language What style of language did the writer use? Notice the words, notice the jargon, and notice the abbreviations	I notice . . . the language is really casual. I wonder . . . why he is so casual with the language? He uses "brekky" to talk about breakfast. Does this tell me something about his audience?

READ WIDELY AND APPLY ANALYSIS SKILLS

After you model, it's time for students to use texts they have selected to complete the notice and wonder protocol. Have them select three or four samples of writing from a career they might be interested in pursuing.

Here are a few examples of the type of workplace writing you could offer, including guidance documents, and you can find many more by searching the Internet:

- Gardening blogs for future gardeners: http://bit.ly/3yMioTP

- Media pitch guide for future business marketers: http://bit.ly/3lgl8G9

- Diet recommendations for future nutritionists: http://bit.ly/3LwitCA

If they are not sure of their career options, have students select articles on topics they find interesting.

Ask them to complete the Notice-and-Wonder Graphic Organizer as they read. When finished, ask students to share with a peer who asks them questions such as:

- Who was the author?

- What was their purpose?

- How did you know this?

- Who is the audience?

- How did you know?

- What are you still wondering about?

After addressing these questions, invite students to add any new insights they gained from the conversation. Next, students can place the analyzed examples in a personal portfolio that can be referred to as a model to help them gain confidence using the *Notice and Wonder* organizer.

When students are preparing to write their own letters, reviews, blogs, or other types of writing, have them complete reviews, using the notice-and-wonder protocol, of a few examples of writing from the genre in which they plan to write. This focuses them on the purpose they are driving forward in their own writing.

SUM IT UP

Just to recap—use the flowchart shown in Figure 6.1 as you develop lesson plans that guide students to think about purpose using the three areas discussed: (1) identifying models, (2) examining models in a structured way, and (3) reading widely and applying analysis skills.

We hope you feel confident and ready to guide your students to use models; to learn about purpose, audience, language, evidence and structure, and revision; and to write in your classroom and way beyond high school. While we have focused on workplace writing, the concepts of gathering models that exemplify the kind of writing to be accomplished, examining them in a structured way, and reading widely to apply analysis skills can work for any kind of writing circumstance. One student might become an informed citizen writing to a congressperson about the airport expansion a mile from their home. One might study to become a marketing specialist for a financial company who's tasked with drafting a pitch. Another might become a nurse practitioner writing a plan for treatment for a patient. The possibilities are wide and deep, but the fact remains, our students will be empowered by having the ability to easily communicate their ideas and thoughts in writing to target audiences. It is an action of equity to teach them how they can support themselves, in whatever writing situation they encounter. Having a voice through writing is every student's right, and it is incumbent on every teacher to teach toward that goal.

PAUSE AND CONSIDER

Revisit the goals you noted at the end of the Introduction of this book. Have they changed? What new goals might you add? What have you learned that you can put into action toward those goals?

Appendices

Example Lesson Plans for Each Phase of Writing

APPLYING IDEAS: A LESSON IN AUDIENCE-FOCUSED RESEARCH

Students in Tami Green's Expository Reading and Writing class are gearing up to begin drafting their proposals for a public rhetoric project. For this project, students are to choose a need or enduring question in their community to research and use to create an argumentative piece. Their aim is to identify a specific audience/stakeholder in their community that will benefit from or act on the research the student has done.

Prior to the lesson detailed in Figure A.1, Ms. Green and her class worked on crafting an annotated bibliography (Figure A.2) with which students would collect their scholarly research and practice MLA format. The class worked on evaluating their research with a specific audience in mind, making sure to address any missing information or deficiencies in their knowledge. From this, students were ready to formally propose their project to the teacher (Figure A.3).

Pay special attention to how Ms. Green used modeling and scaffolds, like sentence frames, to support her students in this multistep process.

Figure B.4 shows a self-assess rubric that students used to evaluate their own efforts to identify and share the purpose for the piece they are writing. The rubric serves as a reminder of what to notice when developing a purpose statement and as a way for students to identify strengths and build in areas that need strengthening.

NOTE: A blank lesson template is available for download on the book's companion website: resources.corwin.com/ClassroomToCareer.

Figure A.1 ◆ Lesson Plan

Completing a Purpose-Driven, Research-Based Proposal for a Targeted Audience
Standards Addressed: CCSS.ELA-LITERACY.W.11-12.8 Gather relevant information from multiple authoritative print and digital sources, using advanced searches effectively; assess the strengths and limitations of each source in terms of the task, purpose, and audience; integrate information into the text selectively to maintain the flow of ideas, avoiding plagiarism and overreliance on any one source and follow a standard format for citation.

Completing a Purpose-Driven, Research-Based Proposal for a Targeted Audience
Purpose Statements: • Content: Finalize and evaluate your research, tailoring it to your specific audience and purpose. • Language: Compose a proposal addressing your research thus far, your intended audience, and the purpose of your project. • Social: Ask for and offer help when needed.

Success Criteria:

"Sum up" my research and write a short paragraph reflecting on how I will use it to address my intended audience and purpose.

Text Used and Rationale:

Claim that seabirds mistake plastic rubbish for food "oversimplified."

Tabitha Watson, *Chemistry World*, June 2017

This text is a scientific article that represents credible, peer-reviewed research that students are expected to use. Additionally, this article's subject matter refutes some of the research I have already found on my topic (for the class example). Using this article provides an opportunity to discuss when it is appropriate, given purpose and audience, to bring in counterclaims and acknowledgement of the opposing viewpoint.

Phase of Learning	Scaffolds/Supports
Show Me: Modeling/Direct Instruction **Share the purpose statements:** - Content: Finalize and evaluate your research, tailoring it to your specific audience and purpose - Language: Compose a proposal addressing your research thus far, your intended audience, and the purpose of your project. - Social: Ask for and offer help when needed ***Show Me: Modeling/Think Aloud*** *Today we are going to revisit the research we have been conducting for our individual stakeholder proposals. As a reminder, we are researching our topics for a specific audience, so everyone will be looking for something a little different. I'm going to show you how I will tailor my current research a little more for my intended audience and purpose. If you want to follow along, I am going to first look at my annotated bibliography to review my research thus far. I'll give you a few moments to access our shared folder if you like.* *My research, as you can see, is on the effects of plastics in the ocean. My proposed audience is San Diego City Council. My purpose is to convince them that single-use plastics—like straws—are harming San Diego's water system. I want the city council to take action to ban straws and plastic lids.* *I notice that all of my research so far is focused on why these plastics are harmful. That seems to make sense, since that is what I am arguing, right? The truth is, I need to remind myself of who my audience is. The city council will probably have members that don't want to alienate or anger businesses that sell or rely on single-use plastics. They will probably have questions for me and may*	Students will see a projected copy of the teacher's text as the teacher conducts a think-aloud; copies will be provided to students per their IEPs or preference. Since the purpose of the think-aloud is to generally share why this is an appropriate article to use, it is not necessary to share copies of the article class-wide. The teacher should circulate around the room and help students get into the shared documents. If technology use is limited, pairs may share a device. Additionally, students may view teacher work on a projector screen if technology use is a distractor for some. Students may review the sample annotated bibliography to see both the sources found and the format used. (Figure A.2 "Sample Annotated Bibliography) Point out how you can quickly see the type of source by using the annotation portion of the annotated bibliography. Depending on teacher resources, you may choose to tailor this to your site's research capabilities. Teacher should write/chart these on the board. Some students may benefit from this list pre-printed for them to check off using their annotated bibliographies.

(Continued)

(Continued)

Phase of Learning	Scaffolds/Supports
even disagree with me. For this reason, I need to find evidence I can use to build a counterclaim. That will allow me to refute this information, which makes my ideas stronger and also adds credibility. *For today, I need to add another source to help me develop my counterclaim and rebuttal. I am still working on using credible sources, so I am going to use the online library search tools to help me find credible sources.* *You'll see that I found an article called* **"Claim that seabirds mistake plastic rubbish for food 'oversimplified'"** *to help strengthen my research. If you check out my annotated bibliography, you'll see that I got this from Chemistry World, which is a credible source; it also has information that my opposition might try to use against my argument. I will use this to make sure my audience feels like I have done my research and am not overly biased.* *I am going to make a list of the ideas I want to consider when I look at my research to help me ensure it is comprehensive before I begin writing my proposal. I need to ask myself:* • *Are my sources credible (do they come from trusted sources my audience will respect)?* • *Did I vet the authors of my research?* • *Did I pull research from a wide range of sources (news articles, scientific studies, personal stories, documentaries, journals, books, etc.)?* • *Did I consider the concerns of my opposition and find evidence to help address those concerns?* *Are there any others I should add?*	
Help Me: Guided Practice *Now I would like you to take a moment to check your own annotated bibliography to see if there are any 'holes' in your research. You might choose to use the list I generated on the board to help guide your thinking.* *Now that we've checked our sources, we can start the proposal drafting process. Please access the "Stakeholder Proposal Sample" on our shared folder. This is where you will use your annotated bibliography to draft your proposal. You may use the sentence frames if you prefer.*	Circulate around the class and offer prompts and cues using the following tools: • The list on the board • Teacher sample annotated bibliography Assist small groups as needed; when students finish, they may begin to draft their proposal if necessary. Alternatively, these can be printed for students to access. (See Figure A.3, "Stakeholder Proposal Planning Sheet") Students have a choice whether to use the frames when writing; they may also choose to use some frames and not others.

Phase of Learning	Scaffolds/Supports
Let Us: Collaboration Before you begin writing, I am going to have you discuss with your partner what you will put in the proposal first. Please use the sentence frames for the first section (topic) to have a discussion with your partner. Take turns using the frames and ask questions when you need clarification.	Students should be seated in heterogeneous groups of two; depending on need, sentence frames may be used to help students ask questions of one another. Circulate around the class and offer prompts and cues using the following tools: • Cueing to the sentence frames when conversation lulls. • Encouraging students to advance to the next section of the organizer if they finish their conversations about each section.
Let Me: Independent *Now that you've practiced reviewing your research and discussing your project with your partner, it is time to write. Notice that you did a lot of talking and reviewing before you got to the writing process—this way of continually drafting is meant to prepare you to conduct longer projects and use your peers and colleagues to help you flesh out your ideas.* *If you finish writing early, make sure you use the sample and our reference books to make sure your paper is formatted correctly; you may also solicit feedback from another peer who is finished. I will be circulating to assist if needed.* Students will use the frames to compose a proposal for their research. Finally, students should complete the self-assessment (Figure B.4)	Sentence frames may be provided to help students get started. A model response may also be provided. The teacher may choose to pull a small group for this section if there are writers needing more support.

Figure A.2 ◆ Sample Annotated Bibliography

Sample Excerpt: Annotated Bibliography

Alvarez, John. *The Plastic Problem*. Revolution Press: San Diego, 2017.

This source gives an in-depth look at how the effects of single-use plastics specifically affect teens. I plan to use this book to show my audience (the city council) that the single-use plastic epidemic is threatening to ruin my and my peers' future and hopefully build some sympathy. This source will help me show how actions made by older generations have affected me and how people my age can help solve the problem.

Kerlin, Kat. "Why Do Seabirds Eat Plastic? The Answer Stinks." *UC Davis*, 17 Nov. 2016, www.ucdavis.edu/news/why-do-seabirds-eat-plastic-answer-stinks/.

This science article on the UC Davis website discusses the effect of plastics on sea life, particularly birds like seagulls. This source combines scientific research and data and breaks it down into "digestible" chunks for a more general audience. It explains the trash problem from the "organisms' perspective" so we can see how this issue harms our sea life.

Watson, Tabitha. "Claim that seabirds mistake plastic rubbish for food 'oversimplified.'" *Chemistry World*, June 2017.

This is an article in a peer-reviewed online journal; it refutes the evidence that plastics are as destructive as previously agreed on. I chose this text because it is a direct response to the article above ("Why do Seabirds Eat Plastic?") and will help me address the concerns of my audience. One of the most important ideas in this source was that the data collected in UC Davis's study could be inaccurate because of the regions used to calculate the effect on birds.

Figure A.3 ◆ Stakeholder Proposal Planning Sheet

Gemma Johnson

Professor Green

Expository Writing

13 December 2018

Stakeholder Proposal

Topic: I chose to explore the topic of ___________ because ___________. I consider this topic to fit under the description of a "hidden story" because ___________. I am particularly interested in this topic because ___________ and hope to gain ___________ out of conducting this research and writing this paper.

Audience (Stakeholder): I have chosen to gear my research and writing toward ___________. This particular group interests me because ___________. My audience has ___________ to gain by reading my research because ___________. I hope to accomplish___________ for my stakeholders. I will know I made an impact when ___________.

Annotated Bibliography: Below please find my research on ___________. I chose the following types of sources to satisfy my audience: ___________. These sources are appropriate because ___________. ___________ about my research surprised me because ___________. A challenge I faced in my research was ___________. I may need to find more sources on ___________ because ___________.

Figure A.4 ◆ Self-Assessment Rubric

Teacher Name: _________________________________

Student Name: _________________________________

Category	3	2	1
Annotated bibliography format	Committing two or fewer errors, I used MLA formatting, at least three credible references from varied sources to create an annotated bibliography on my topic.	Committing three or fewer errors, I used MLA formatting and at least three credible references to create an annotated bibliography on my topic.	I attempted to use MLA format to create an annotated bibliography on my topic but: • Used fewer than three sources • Committed four or more errors • Used nonacademic sources
Proposal	I completed all three parts of the proposal, moving beyond the sentence frames to ensure my work was complete and unique to my voice, with no grammatical errors.	I completed all three parts of the proposal, using the sentence frames to ensure my work was complete with no distracting grammatical errors.	I am missing one or more parts of the proposal, and/or I have distracting and major grammatical errors in my writing.
Research methods	I used a variety of sources that are appropriate to my audience, including multiple sources that consider the opposition. I have thoroughly vetted and cross-checked the information from my sources.	I used a variety of sources that are appropriate to my audience, including a source that considers the opposition. I may have one or two sources that need more vetting or corroboration with other sources.	I have referenced multiple sources that may contain misinformation, may not be appropriate for my audience, or may be from similar resources.

Appendix B

Below is a plan from Miss Kate Sezane's high school history class, where students take part in a lesson intended to get them writing with a focus on civics (Figure B.1). Miss Sezane wants her students to feel confident and empowered to have a voice in politics and social developments at the community, state, or even national level. She knows that her students feel challenged by the language they hear from politicians and lawmakers, so Miss Sezane wants to show them how to decode using a notable model speech made by Senator Margaret Chase Smith in the 1950s.

Using a teacher think-aloud, which is presented in detail within the lesson, Miss Sezane articulates her thinking so that students can see what she is noticing as she comments about language and structure choices seen in the speech. Figure B.2 details Miss Sezane's scripted think-aloud. Miss Sezane planned her think-aloud in advance so that she could target areas that aligned with her lesson purpose in an intentional manner. Notice that Miss Sezane even planned her annotations. Annotations document the thinking as Miss Sezane reads and thinks aloud for her class.

Following this, students practice thinking aloud about the model, noticing tone, vocabulary, and other elements of the speech that make it compelling. Miss Sezane knows that chunking the text and having students participate in partner talk in between each read chunk are essential to deepening understanding. She offers students sentence frames (Figure B.3) to scaffold this partner talk.

The next step is to let students practice using another model speech to notice language choices, style, and tone. Miss Sezane even provides students with a self-assessment rubric, so they can evaluate their progress in using a model text (Figure B.4). The rubric serves as a reminder of what to notice when looking at a model and as a way for students to identify strengths and build in areas that need strengthening.

After lots of practice using these models, Miss Sezane uses the writing strategy RAFT (R–role, A–audience, F–format, T–topic) to guide her students in small groups as they write from the perspective of senators with a point to make. Understanding the use of models is Miss Sezane's teaching aim, and as a part of that, she models how to use models—a delightful irony!

NOTE: A blank lesson template is available for download on the book's companion website: resources.corwin.com/ClassroomToCareer

Figure B.1 • Lesson Plan

Lesson Focus: Modeling and Thinking Aloud About Speech Writing

Standards Addressed:

CCSS.ELA-LITERACY.W.9-10.9 Draw evidence from literary or informational texts to support analysis, reflection, and research – Writing Standard.

History-Social Science Content Standards: Historical Research, Evidence, and Point of View—Students evaluate major debates among historians concerning alternative interpretations of the past, including an analysis of authors' use of evidence and the distinctions between sound generalizations and misleading oversimplifications.

Purpose Statements:

- Content: Identify elements that make a speech strong and compelling by accessing a model text.

- Language: Notice the language, tone, and style choices made by the author of a compelling speech so that I can create my own.

- Social: Share ideas with partners and to listen to partner's ideas.

Lesson Focus: Modeling and Thinking Aloud About Speech Writing

Success Criteria:

I can use stylistic and language elements that make a speech strong and compelling.

Text Used and Rationale:

Smith, Margaret Chase. Remarks to the Senate in Support of a Declaration of Conscience. (1950)

- This text is found in appendix B of the CCSS-ELA, 9th-10th grade information text exemplar and is known as an example of a strong, compelling speech within a historical context.

Scan the QR code to read Margaret Chase Smith's remarks to the Senate (1950)

Phase of Learning	Scaffolds/Supports
Show Me: Modeling/Direct Instruction **Share the purpose statements:** - Content: Identify elements that make a speech strong and compelling - Language: Notice the language and structural choices made by the author of a compelling speech - Social: Share ideas with partners and listen to partner's ideas Teacher will think aloud about the first few sections of Margaret Chase Smith's **Remarks to the Senate in Support of a Declaration of Conscience** utilizing a think-aloud script that shows how to notice these elements: vocabulary used, tone, sentence structure, and content. See think-aloud script (Figure C.2).	- Provide students with text for annotating. - Think aloud about elements that might be confusing to students (confusing vocabulary, audience being addressed, context, and background) - Annotate using a document camera so that students can see your modeling of how to make notes about your thinking while reading. - Provide historical information to build context (https://www.senate.gov/artandhistory/history/common/generic/Featured_Bio_SmithMargaret.htm) if needed. - Move around the classroom during partner talk. Prompt, cue, and ask questions when students struggle with sharing annotations with partners (i.e., Why did you annotate this word? How did the author set the tone? What words might you underline to connect the tone?).

Phase of Learning	Scaffolds/Supports
Students will annotate their copies of the speech, identifying what the teacher notices and adding any other annotations they deem appropriate. After the think-aloud, students will share their annotations with a partner and explain any additional annotations they have made. Bring class together to share with the whole group. Be sure students notice how the teacher thinks aloud about tone, language, and style.	
Help Me: Guided Practice Teacher prompts students to read and annotate the next section of the text by offering this direction—*Underline important ideas and write in the margins why they are important. Circle confusing words and see if you can use the context to predict meaning. Use a short comment and question mark to show where you are confused. Notice tone and document what you think it might be.* Text: It is ironical that we Senators can in debate in the Senate directly or indirectly, by any form of words, impute to any American who is not a Senator any conduct or motive unworthy or unbecoming an American—and without that non-Senator American having any legal redress against us—yet if we say the same thing in the Senate about our colleagues we can be stopped on the grounds of being out of order. After students have annotated and documented their thinking, have them read aloud and share their thoughts with a partner. Use the sentence frames (Figure B.3) to talk about the text with a partner. Teacher then prompts whole class discussion: What ideas did you have in common? What did you see your partner noticed that you didn't? Repeat guided practice activity with 1 or 2 more sections of the text.	• Move around the classroom and listen in to notice where students were confused. Provide scaffolded questions to help them consider areas of confusion (How is the speaker comparing senators with other Americans? What's the connection between *dropped* and *out of order*? • Share a photo of the speaker and audience to help build context. • Provide vocabulary information if students need support (*impute, unbecoming, redress*) but only after students have independently tried to figure these words out.
Let Us: Collaboration Have students use another model text—for example, read: Scan the QR code to read Everett M. Dirksen's remarks to the Senate on the Civil Rights Bill (1964)	• Provide a current speech about an issue that Congress is currently addressing. • Move among students to observe their annotations and sharing of ideas. When students are stuck, prompt and cue to help them think about elements of a speech (What tone do you want to use? What language will convey that tone?) • Show a model of a RAFT for a different speech.

(Continued)

(Continued)

Phase of Learning	Scaffolds/Supports
Or a speech about a current issue that Congress is dealing with – Resources: Scan the QR code to view a list of classic Senate speeches. Scan the QR code to view Congress' list of most-viewed bills. Students work with a partner to annotate the text. They may again use the sentence frames provided to support their partner work (Figure B.3). Next, have students write a collaborative RAFT with a partner or small group. RAFT is an acronym that stands for **Role, Audience, Format,** and **Topic.** **R- Role** – you are a group of senators **A - Audience** – fellow members of Congress and the president **F- Format** – Brief written mini-speech to be delivered to congress using appropriate vocabulary, tone, and content. **T- Topic** – Why we support (or don't support) the Natural Resources Management Act (or whatever bill is chosen: Once students are finished, have them share their mini-speech with another group. Each listening group should share what they notice about the **language used, the tone, and the content.** Students provide feedback to the partner group on these elements.	
Let Me: Independent Have students write a brief exit slip that goes back to the purpose statements: • Content: Identify elements that make a speech strong and compelling by **accessing a model text**.	

Phase of Learning	Scaffolds/Supports
• Language: Notice the language, tone, and style choices made by the author of a compelling speech so that I can create my own. • Social: Share ideas with partners and listen to partner's ideas. Exit Slip: *What did you notice about the language, tone, and style of Margaret Chase Smith's speech? What elements of language, tone, and style did you include in your speech? Explain your responses. How did using a model help you to think about these elements of a speech?*	• Have students return to their annotations of Smith's speech. • Remind them to return to their other model text and their RAFT to think about language, tone, and style. • Suggest to students that tone can be serious, light, funny, passionate, stern, friendly, etc. • Remind students that language can be formal, informal, technical, colloquial, etc. • Share examples of various text structures so that students are aware that sentence structure can be short and to the point, explanatory, complex, with bullet points, etc. • Remind them to notice what's in the model text and to annotate. Post pictures of annotated texts for students to reference.

Figure B.2 • Miss Sezane's Plan for a Think-Aloud, as Noted in Her Lesson Plan

Think-Aloud for Remarks to the Senate in Support of a Declaration of Conscience

Text	Think Aloud – What the Teacher Articulates to Show Thinking
Remarks to the Senate in Support of a Declaration of Conscience, Margaret Chase Smith (1950)	I see that the title of this is **Remarks to the Senate in Support of a Declaration of Conscience**. I'm not sure what that title means, but I think remarks are comments or thoughts about a topic. The word declaration reminds me of the Declaration of Independence, which we learned about previously in this class. It's when the author stated their ideas about becoming a free nation. I wonder if declaration is the same here? Stating ideas? I see this is written in 1950, so this is in the past. I'm going to try to put myself into the 1950s as I read this. Interesting that it's written by a woman before the Civil Rights Movement and Women's Liberation Movement was in full swing. Ok. I'm going to read this.
Mr. President: I would like to speak briefly and simply about a serious national condition. It is a national feeling of fear and frustration that could result in national suicide and the end of everything that we Americans hold dear. It is a condition that comes from the lack of effective leadership in either the Legislative Branch or the Executive Branch of our Government.	Teacher reads text and thinks about these elements: I see this is being addressed to the president. I wonder if it's a political speech? "National condition"– she says she has a "feeling of **frustration and fear**." Those are emotional terms. It must be a tough time in history. She sounds **passionate and concerned**. She's calling out ineffective leadership. I wonder why?

(Continued)

(Continued)

Text	Think Aloud – What the Teacher Articulates to Show Thinking
That leadership is so lacking that serious and responsible proposals are being made that national advisory commissions be appointed to provide such critically needed leadership.	"Commissions" – I think those are groups of people that focus on certain areas. **The language and tone are very formal.**
I speak as briefly as possible because too much harm has already been done with irresponsible words of bitterness and selfish political opportunism. I speak as briefly as possible because the issue is too great to be obscured by eloquence. I speak simply and briefly in the hope that my words will be taken to heart.	She's **repeating the idea** that she's speaking briefly. I say that at the start of this speech. I see she's saying "selfish political opportunism." Simply and briefly—**there's that repetition again.**
I speak as a Republican. I speak as a woman. I speak as a United States Senator. I speak as an American.	These are short phrases. They sound strong and powerful. I know she's a Republican and a Senator. She ends with "I speak as an American." That sounds like she's speaking for everyone or at least she says she is.
The United States Senate has long enjoyed worldwide respect as the greatest deliberative body in the world. But recently that deliberative character has too often been debased to the level of a forum of hate and character assassination sheltered by the shield of congressional immunity.	I don't know what "deliberative means," but it says that the US has respect. She says "but"– that's a signal word that shows contrast. Next it says something about "hate and character assassination." That sounds negative. So first she says we have respect, but now she says there's "hate and character assassination." Those are conflicting ideas. Congressional immunity – not sure what that is, but when you have immunity to a disease it means you don't get sick. I wonder if she's saying that people in Congress can get protected, like protection from an illness. I'll have to keep going to see if I'm on target here.

Figure B.3 • Sentence Frames to Support the Use of Models

The title makes me think ________________.

When I look at this sentence, I notice ________________.

Based on my understanding of the author's purpose, ________________.

The tone suggests ________________.

I'm not sure what this word (or sentence) means, however, I will ________________.

The text structure shows ________________.

The language used by the author indicates ________________.

Figure B.4 • Student Self-Assessment Rubric

Student Name: _________________________________

Category	3	2	1
Key elements of a model text are identified	Annotations of model text indicate deep understanding of *audience, language, tone,* and *style.*	Annotations of model text indicate some understanding of *audience, language, tone,* and *style.*	Annotations of model text indicate weak understanding of *audience, language, tone,* and *style.*
Key elements of model text are utilized in student authored text	My written text addresses *audience, language, tone,* and style in a similar manner to the model text.	My written text addresses *audience, language, tone,* and style in a somewhat similar manner to the model text.	My written text addresses *audience, language, tone,* and style in a different manner to the model text.
Identification of how a model supports writing.	I can clearly explain, with examples, how noticing elements of a model text supports my own writing in a similar workplace situation.	I can somewhat explain, with some examples, how noticing elements of a model text supports my own writing in a similar workplace situation.	I can weakly explain, with few or no examples, how noticing elements of a model text supports my own writing in a similar workplace situation.

APPLYING IDEAS: A LOOK AT THE LANGUAGE USED BY WORKPLACE WRITERS

In Mr. Cory Watson's English classroom, students are grappling with the use of language to communicate in various workplace and academic settings. They know that an online magazine reporter documenting the latest developments in Washington, D.C., will write using different language than an electrician might use to communicate wiring plans; however, students don't quite know how to pinpoint what kind of language is best in certain situations. To move students towards a critical understanding of the range of language used and the underpinnings that motivate writer choices, Mr. Watson engages his class in a lesson that guides them to connect with those that work and write in various environments (see Figure C.1).

Students interview professionals to get a better understanding of the varied ways in which writing is used in the workplace.

Scan the QR code to access student interviews of professionals from The Disciplinary Literacy Interview Project.

Of course, Mr. Watson shares a model interview, so that students can see how to ask questions. To help guide students toward the development of strong interview questions and useful replies, Mr. Watson models how to conduct an interview with a workplace professional. This example in Figure C.2 is from an interview with a hospital nurse. Using this model helps students to compose their own questions and guides them to dig deeper when responses are too short or superficial.

Once they have collected their interview data, Mr. Watson employs a compare/contrast activity using an interview analysis guide, done in small groups, to promote a more profound understanding of how writing can vary, depending upon the circumstance and the need (Figure 3.3). Students compare the elements of their own interviews with those of two other students. This comparison helps them to identify how writing differs and/or is similar in various situations. It is the attention to the differences and similarities that helps students understand what elements they might notice when encountering a future workplace scenario. Students summarize their thoughts in an exit slip format, using provided sentence frames if needed.

To further extend understanding of language in writing, Mr. Watson, has students use a self-analysis rubric to explore aspects of texts provided by professionals and to use when they compose their own workplace writing examples (Figure C.4). Below is the rubric that Mr. Watson shares with his students as they examine samples of workplace writing. Students are directed to notice the clarity of the purpose, the organization, and the use of vocabulary, structure, and conventions. Sometimes Mr. Watson will provide students with a weakly composed text just so they can identify what might make it a better, stronger communication. Students also refer to this rubric when writing their own text. It's a valuable tool for composing and evaluating texts.

Understanding how language can convey a message in various ways is essential to success on the job or in the classroom. Mr. Watson's students clearly realize this!

NOTE: A blank lesson template is available for download on the book's companion website: resources.corwin.com/ClassroomToCareer.

Figure C.1 • Lesson Plan

Lesson Focus: What's the Best Way to Express Myself in a Workplace Situation
Standards Addressed: CCSS-ELA Writing 4. Produce clear and coherent writing in which the development, organization, and style are appropriate to task, purpose, and audience. CCSS-ELA Language 3. Apply knowledge of language to understand how language functions in different contexts, to make effective choices for meaning or style, and to comprehend more fully when reading or listening.
Purpose Statements: • Content: Identify and use elements of language in writing to address a specified audience in a specific context. • Language: Consider audience needs, language registers, and language variety when writing to a specific audience. • Social: Work with a partner by sharing ideas in a respectful, collegial manner.
Success Criteria: **I can identify and use appropriate language elements when writing to a specific audience.**
Text Used and Rationale: Students will look at sample texts from three professions: • Notes from a college student in a geology class preparing for a presentation. • A script for a commercial, developed by writers pitching an idea to clients. • An inventory list for a beauty salon that needs to restock their products for sale to the public and their products for internal use by beauticians. • Other workplace texts may also be used.

Phase of Learning	Scaffolds/Supports
Show Me: Modeling/Direct Instruction The teacher selects a professional to interview and then models how to craft interview questions that focus on writing and the language of the profession. The teacher shares an interview response from a professional. Figure C.2 is a nurse's interview response. Using the *Interview Analysis Guide*, the teacher models how to analyze the same interview (Figure C.3).	• Teacher models how to craft interview questions such as the following: *What kind of writing do you do in your profession?* *When you write to your work colleagues or your clients, what are the topics you discuss?* *Are there special words or terms that you use?* *How are you learning the language of your profession?*

(Continued)

(Continued)

Phase of Learning	Scaffolds/Supports
	Do you use different language or phrases in different situations? (for example, when writing to a coworker vs. writing to other people you work with like clients) • Teacher uses a sample interview (figure C.2) to show how to analyze the interview and then documents the analysis using the tool *interview analysis guide* (figure C.3)
Help Me: Guided Practice Teacher provides a contact list of professionals who have agreed to be interviewed. Alternatively, the website: **https://literacybeat.com/literacy-in-the-disciplines/** (Lapp, D. & Wolsey, T.D. Literacy in the Disciplines, April, 2016) has interviews with professionals who discuss writing in their fields. Students could access this to consider how writing is used in technology and entertainment, the arts, engineering, and in science. If access to professionals is limited, the teacher could provide interview data that the teacher has already collected.	• Provide a copy of Figure C.3 *interview Analysis Guide* for students to use when analyzing their own interviews. • Monitor student progress and provide scaffolded questions when needed (*What do you notice about her language in this response to the interview question? How is writing to her colleagues different from writing to patients?*) • Share the teacher model again with students that struggle.

Let Us: Collaboration
 	
In groups of three, students will share their interview analysis data and will compare with their partners by discussing and documenting *what's similar* and *what's different* in their charts.
	• Monitor student groups and provide prompts, cues, or questions to promote thinking and collaboration (*How is the way the nurse learned the language of nursing similar or different to how the bank teller learned her profession's language?*)
	
	• Provide sentence frames to help students engage in conversations
	   o Could you share your data about _____?
	   o I'm not sure I understand _____.
	   o Based on what you stated about your interview, I think _____.

Let Me: Independent
 	
Teacher provides students with a chance to synthesize and consolidate their understandings of writing in various professions by having them respond to this exit slip prompt:
 	
• After analyzing writing and sharing analyses with partners, what can you conclude about learning to write in any profession? Why is it important?
 	
• How could you use your understanding of writing in the professions you explored to help develop your own writing?
	• Provide sentence starters to help students build academic language and to get them started with their exit slip task:
	   o After analyzing with my partners, I conclude that _____.
	   o Based on my understanding of writing in the workplace _____
	   o The interview analysis showed me that _____.
	   o I can use what I learned to _____.
	   o Now I plan to _____.
	   o My analysis makes me realize _____.

Figure C.2 • Interview With Nurse, Mary Alexander, Who Works in an Urban Hospital That Serves a Diverse Community.

What kind of writing do you do in your profession?

I document patient responses to treatments, monitoring of conditions, and other notes on patient charts. I also write emails to colleagues and keep notes for other nurses that take over after my shift is finished. The notes are kept with a computer program that we update. I also keep my own notes, so that I can more easily chart the information.

When you write to your work colleagues or your clients, what are the topics you discuss?

We discuss patient care, community needs, timely matters of health care in our hospital, and other workplace issues like head-to-toe assessment of patients and the patient plan, which is what the doctor has planned. We might also discuss family needs or cultural needs of the patient.

Are there special words or terms that you use? How are you learning the language of your profession?

Oh yes! We no longer write abbreviations for conditions or patient vitals, because they are not universal and can cause confusion. We instead write whole terms and explanations. We also have technical language that we use. I work in telemetry and use terms like septic, pneumonia, and stroke. We might talk about a deficit that a stroke patient has when one side of their body is weak or has impaired strength. We use the phrase "alert and oriented' to describe a patient's current condition when we are assessing their baseline. It gets very technical. If I'm communicating with a patient, I have to explain more clearly what these terms mean. If I'm connecting with a coworker, a doctor, or nurse, we can use our medical language, and we all understand. Communication can be faster that way. I learned much of the language I need in nursing school. Some of it I learned when I was a biology major in college. Mostly that was anatomy and physiology terms. Nursing school required use of technical and clinical language. I had lots of writing tasks in nursing school that focused on medical scenarios, and I had to respond in writing using medical terms. I've also learned some language on the job. In the telemetry department, there are specific words and phrases I've picked up.

Do you use different language or phrases in different situations?

Yes. To add more to what I mentioned about patient and coworker language differences, here are some other thoughts. When I discuss conditions or illnesses with patients, I have to carefully select my words. I have to be sensitive to their feelings. They could be dealing with the emotions of having just been diagnosed with a heart condition. Or I could be communicating with kids who have just lost a parent. Sensitivity and compassion are very important when choosing the right language to use with our patients. With other nurses or doctors, time is often an issue and we need to be efficient and thorough. That's when my notes and charting use the accepted medical terms and I have to be very accurate and very attentive to this kind of writing. I have to document all patient care and needs.

Figure C.3 • Interview Analysis Guide—Compare and Contrast Writing

	My Interview	Partner 1's Interview	Partner 2's Interview	What's Similar	What's different
Profession	nursing				
Type of writing	• Charting of patient conditions and other information • Notes for colleagues				

(Continued)

(Continued)

	My Interview	Partner 1's Interview	Partner 2's Interview	What's Similar	What's different
Topics	• Patient care • Community needs • Timely matters of healthcare • Workplace issues (family needs, cultural needs, etc).				
Special terms or words used	• Technical language – deficit, stroke, septic, alert and oriented				
How to learn the language of the profession or job	• Biology studies in college • Nursing school • Some on the job in telemetry dept.				
How language is different in different situations	• With other doctors, use medical terms – precise and accurate • With patients, compassionate language and lots of explanation				

Figure C.4 • Self-Assess the Use of Language in Writing.

Student Name: ______________________________

Category	3	2	1
Purpose of the communication	Communicates the message; includes many of the details that are clearly connected to the details of the message.	Communicates the message; includes some of the details that are connected to the message but includes some irrelevant information.	Weakly communicates the message; includes few details which are loosely connected; there is much irrelevant information.
Organization	The message is logical and coherent in its sequence which moves from beginning to middle to end. Smooth transition among ideas.	The message is logical in its sequence which moves from beginning to middle to end. Transitions are limited.	Sequence of the message is unclear. Transitions are abrupt and unclear. Contains disconnected ideas.

Category	3	2	1
Vocabulary	Includes a wide array of work related vocabulary that addresses the intent of the message.	Includes a variety of work related vocabulary that is somewhat related to the message.	Work-related vocabulary is unrelated to the general message; or work-related vocabulary is not included.
Structure and conventions	Message contains a high degree of control of subject-verb agreement, tense, noun-adjective agreement, word order, spelling, and punctuation.	Message contains some control of subject-verb agreement, tense, noun-adjective agreement, word order, spelling, and punctuation.	Message contains a limited control of subject-verb agreement, tense, noun-adjective agreement, word order, spelling, and punctuation.
Addressing the audience	Uses language register and language variety that are appropriate for the intended audience.	Uses language register and language variety that are somewhat appropriate for the intended audience.	Uses language register and language variety that are inappropriate for the intended audience.

Appendix D

APPLYING IDEAS: A LESSON IN TEXT FEATURES

Scarlett Jimenez and her 10th grade Public Health students are currently studying epidemiology and using Mark Preston's novel *The Hot Zone* to enrich their understanding of Ebola, how it spreads, and the representation of infectious diseases in literature and popular culture. To accompany their novel study, Ms. Jimenez and her students are exploring how different mediums address and discuss Ebola. In the following lesson, Ms. Jimenez is leading her students through a lesson on text features and their effects on an author's purpose and audience. Because her students will soon be writing their own expository pieces on an infectious disease for a specific audience, Ms. Jimenez wanted to provide an opportunity for them to understand how a model text works from the inside out. Read the lesson shared as Figure D.1 to see how she and her class tackled this reading task. The graphic organizers shown in Figures D.2–D.4 can be used as scaffolds for noticing, analyzing, and planning text features.

Figure D.5 is a self-assessment rubric that students may use to evaluate the structure and support they used when making a claim. The rubric serves as a reminder of what to notice when looking at a claim and as a way for students to identify strengths and add to areas that need strengthening.

NOTE: A blank lesson template is available for download on the book's companion website: resources.corwin.com/ClassroomToCareer.

Figure D.I • Lesson Plan

Lesson Focus: Identifying Text Features Using Think-Aloud and "Notice and Wonder" Protocol
Standards Addressed: CCSS.ELA–LITERACY.RI.9–I0.6   Determine an author's point of view or purpose in a text and analyze how an author uses rhetoric to advance that point of view or purpose.
Purpose Statements: • Content: Examine how text features and structures contribute to a text's overall meaning and purpose   • Language: Use concrete evidence from the text to support your thinking; make inferences and ask questions based on the evidence you examined   • Social: Share your ideas with a partner and reach consensus
Success Criteria: **Correctly identify text features and explain how they demonstrate an author's purpose and audience.**

> ***Text Used and Rationale:***
>
> "How Ebola Spread Out of Control," ***Washington Post***
>
> Story by: Lena Sun, Brady Dennis, Lenny Bernstein, Joel Achenbach
>
> Photos by: Michel du Cille
>
> Published on October 4, 2014
>
> 
>
> Scan the QR code to read the article "How Ebola
> Spread Out of Control" (*Washington Post*)
>
> This text is taught in tandem with **The Hot Zone** by Mark Preston, a Common Core text exemplar. This article has multiple text features and "real-world" writing techniques to showcase and connect to the class novel.

Phase of Learning	Scaffolds/Supports
Show Me: Modeling/Direct Instruction **Share the purpose statements:** • Content: Examine how text features and structures contribute to a text's overall meaning and purpose • Language: Use concrete evidence from the text to support your thinking; make inferences and ask questions based on the evidence you examined • Social: Share your ideas with a partner and note areas where you agreed and disagreed.	Students will get access to their own copy of the text.* *For this reading, digital access is preferred, as many of the text features are unique to an online environment. If needed, the article can be printed, but be aware that not all text features will "work." The teacher should circulate the room and help students get onto the article; if technology use is limited, pairs may share a device.
Modeling/Think Aloud: *Today we are going to continue to learn about the Ebola virus, the topic of our class novel study in* <u>The Hot Zone</u>. *Our goal today is to be able to use annotations and conversations to explain how an article we might read in the newspaper explores this topic and uses common text features to give us insight into the purpose and audience. Let me give you a moment to access today's article on our class web page.* *You'll see that this is the article we read last night for homework; today we will take a close look at some of the "extras" the author put in to help us better understand the article and keep us interested. I am going to demonstrate in a few moments how to find these "extras," what they are called, and what clues they can give me about the author's main purpose, as well as the audience.*	Additionally, students may view teacher work on a projector screen if technology use is a distractor for some. Having students be already familiar with the piece will make it easier for them to comprehend the material and focus on the text features themselves. Students needing more support with the article also met in a reading group prior to today's lesson to ensure they understood the content overall. Hand out the graphic organizer (Figure D.2) to students in case they want to take notes; they should also take out figure D.3 to help them identify features. The teacher should, if possible, project the article onto a screen or whiteboard so students can see along with her while she thinks aloud.

(Continued)

(Continued)

Phase of Learning	Scaffolds/Supports
While I think about this, I am going to take notes using a study skill we've been practicing—notice and wonder. I'll track my thoughts on the "Notice and Wonder graphic organizer" (Figure D.2) and also have my "Common Text Structures and Features" (Figure D.3) handout from last week on hand in case I forget what the features are. *Since my goal is to examine features and how they relate to the author's purpose and audience, I am going to scan the article. The first feature that catches my eye are the graphics on page one. The photograph of the young girl lying down immediately draws my attention; if I look down further, I can see the caption that reads "A sick child, Cynthia, waits outside Redemption Hospital in Monrovia, Liberia, for health workers to remove dead bodies before she can enter."* *Well, clearly the author has my attention and my sympathy already! Dead bodies? Children? That's a lot of pathos right there. Let me note this in my graphic organizer. . . . I'm going to write down the feature as "images and captions" and put down page one, so I can find this later if I need to. I think this feature is meant to get my attention and pluck at my heartstrings since the image is so heartbreaking. This makes me think the audience must be "everyday" people like me but maybe also on the older side since the caption hints at a more graphic side to this disease. I also know that sympathy is often used to persuade people, so I know this article can't strictly be aimed at the scientific community. Let me write this down.* *I want to make sure I don't judge all images the same, however. I notice this image further down on the screen looks more like a graph/figure.* *This type of image gives me information about mortality rates and more scientific evidence to support the idea that Ebola is dangerous and devastating. I think I should note this in my graphic organizer; I also think that this gives me more information about the purpose and audience of this article—the use of facts and statistics shows the indisputable damage caused by this epidemic. So, the authors are not only playing on my emotions; they are appealing to my sense of reason and logic by using statistics. I also know not everyone can read figures like these, so it narrows my audience a bit. I think this article is for late teens, like you guys, and up. I also think it's a mixed audience so far because the authors are using multiple appeals here.*	Transition from article on screen to the graphic organizer under a document camera, if available. Students should see the teacher writing their answer as they model how to use the graphic organizer. The teacher may also have students copy into their own graphic organizers so they have a model for the second and third rows. Students should see the teacher writing their answer in as they model how to use the graphic organizer. The teacher may also have students copy into their own graphic organizers so they have a model for the second and third rows. This graphic may also be printed out for more in-depth practice if needed.

Phase of Learning	Scaffolds/Supports
So, to recap, I looked at the first two text features of the article, I named them using my list, and I thought and wrote notes about how they work but also jotted down how they give me insight into the author's purpose and audience. Now, I want us to practice with your partner with the next feature—the graphic on the stages of haemorrhagic fever.	
Help Me: Guided Practice *Now, in your groups, I want you to practice the same thinking and note-taking I did with this new feature:* *Don't forget to note what type of feature it is, where you found it, and what effect it has. We will reconvene as a whole class in a few minutes to share our thinking.* *Ok, now that we have had a chance to think about this feature with our partners, let's get a few volunteers to explain what they discussed and wrote on their graphic organizer.*	Students should be seated in heterogeneous pairs of two; depending on need, sentence frames may be used to help students fill out the next row of the graphic organizer (Figure D.4). Circulate around the class and offer prompts and cues using the following tools: • Cueing to the text features, document, or the first row of the graphic organizer • Sentence frames to help students get their thoughts down on paper (Figure D.4) Since this feature is a mix of graphics, captions, and slides, students may struggle to name it. Encourage them to consider how the format (online article) makes certain features possible. Is there potential for new, never-before-seen features? Reconvening as a class allows the instructor to address common misconceptions about the class, allow students to share their knowledge with other groups to help them flesh out their own ideas, and provides an opportunity for the collaborative task coming up.
Let Us: Collaboration: *Now, I am going to ask your partner and you to join another partnership; together you will fill out the last row of the graphic organizer together. To ramp up the challenge, you **cannot** choose another image or graph as your text feature to analyze. I will be circulating the room to assist. Remember, your goal as a group is to share ideas with your partners and ultimately some to a shared conclusion that you will write your notes on.*	Students should be seated in heterogeneous groups of four; depending on need, sentence frames may be used to help students fill out the next row of the graphic organizer (Figure D.4). Circulate around the class and offer prompts and cues using the following tools: • Cueing to the text features, document, or the first row of the graphic organizer • Sentence frames to help students get their thoughts down on paper (Figure D.4) It may be helpful to catalog the features of the article in case groups are struggling to find more features.

(Continued)

(Continued)

Phase of Learning	Scaffolds/Supports
Let Me: Independent: *Now that you've practiced finding, examining, and talking about text features in this article, I want you to take one more step in thinking about how these features work together to create a meaning. At the bottom of your organizer, you are to explain, using the "Claim, Evidence, and Reasoning" format you use in all of your classes, how the text features you examined today helped establish and further the authors' purpose in this article.* Students will answer the following question in the last field of their graphic organizer: **How did the structures and features of the text further its purpose? Write below, using Claim, Evidence, and Reasoning.** Finally, students should complete the self-assessment (Figure D.5)	Sentence frames may be provided to help students get started. A model response may also be provided (Figure D.4)

Figure D.2 • Notice-and-Wonder Graphic Organizer

Title of Article, Author, and Where to Find It	
Purpose Identify the reason the author is writing this piece. What is the intent?	
Structure identifies the ways in which the author constructs the text. **Were these techniques used?** • flashbacks or flash forwards • literary montage (a few pictures or scenes to tell the story)	I notice . . . I wonder . . .
Title of Article, Author, and Where to Find It	
• vignettes • journaling • chronology If used, were they effective?	
Audience Who is this piece intended for?	I notice . . . I wonder . . .
Language What style of language did the writer use? What style of language did the writer use? Notice the words, notice the jargon, and notice the abbreviations	I notice . . . I wonder . . .

Figure D.3 • Common Text Structures and Features

Common Text Structures	Common Text Features
Descriptive	Headers
Cause and Effect	Captions
Problem and Solution	Graphics/Illustrations
Sequence/Chronological Order	Labels
Compare/Contrast	Subtitles
	Glossary
	Table of Contents
	Index
	Maps
	Special Print/Font

Figure D.4 • Sentence Frames

The following sentence frames were used by Ms. Jimenez to support students' presentation of information they used to make and support their claims.

Sentence Frames for Graphic Organizer	
For Analyzing the Text Features: ________ (name of feature) is located on ________________ (page number). This feature is/does/provides ________________ for the article.	**For Claim, Evidence, and Reasoning:** **Claim:** The use of textual features like ________________ (provide examples here) serves to ________________ (what effect do these features have on the text?).

Sentence Frames for Graphic Organizer	
By including ________________ (name of feature) the author makes the reader ________________ (examples: "think, feel, trust, distrust, wonder, question…."). This happens because ________________ .	Evidence: In ________________ (location of feature/s) of the article, the author ________________ (provide example of feature/describe feature). Reasoning: By ________________ (recap the evidence used above/explain what it does), the argument is strengthened/weakened because ________________ .

Figure D.5 • Self-Assessment Rubric

Teacher Name _______________________________

Student Name _______________________________

Category	3	2	1
Text feature identification	I correctly identified three different types of text features in the article.	I correctly identified two different types of text features in the article.	I identified no text features, or incorrectly identified one or more text features.
Text features and author's purpose	I thoroughly explained how the text feature supports and enhances the author's purpose and reveals their audience.	I explained, but perhaps at a surface-level, how the text feature supports the author's purpose and reveals their audience.	I addressed some but not all of the following: • text feature and how it supports author's purpose • text feature and how it reveals audience.
Claim, evidence, reasoning	I used a claim, direct or paraphrased evidence from the text, and thorough reasoning to explain whether or not the author's use of text features were successful in achieving their purpose.	I used a claim, direct or paraphrased evidence from the text, and simple reasoning to explain whether or not the author's use of text features were successful in achieving their purpose.	I attempted to determine whether the author's use of text features achieved their purpose but was missing one of the following: • Claim • Evidence • Reasoning

APPLYING IDEAS: A LESSON IN FEEDBACK AND PERSONAL SUCCESS CRITERIA

Rich Ramirez is teaching a 9th grade English course that incorporates college and career standards in addition to ELA standards. The focus of his course is writing and reading in the medical field. Currently, his students, who are also interns in local hospitals, are working on revising their drafts of a patient case study. Mr. Ramirez and his class are in the middle of a unit on ethics in medicine; for this assignment, students have been asked to choose a case study in which the medical professionals involved encountered an ethical dilemma around how to deliver treatment (Figure E.1).

Students are expected to choose a case study from *The Cambridge Medical Ethics Handbook* and compose a write-up for an audience of aspiring medical students. They are to include the pertinent details of the case, note the ethical dilemma, and then propose the next best steps using reasoning and ideas from class studied on different philosophies on health care. Mr. Ramirez provides a rubric to guide students' case study write-ups, as shown in Figure E.2.

Mr. Ramirez uses error analysis to collect data on his students' drafts and composed a sample paper to use that reflects the major errors across the class. To see how he used error analysis to plan his lesson in Figures E.3 and E.4.

Finally, Figure E.5 shows a self-assess rubric that students may use to evaluate their own efforts as they edit and revise their writing. The rubric serves as a reminder of what to notice when reviewing a text under construction to identify strengths and build in areas that need strengthening.

Read on to find Mr. Ramirez's lesson (Figure E.1) see how he uses this sample in collaborative groups to help students formulate their approach to their own revisions.

NOTE: A blank lesson template is available for download on the book's companion website: resources.corwin.com/ClassroomToCareer.

Figure E.1 • Lesson Plan

Lesson Focus: Using Samples to Develop a Revision Plan and Personal Success Criteria
Standards Addressed: CCSS.ELA-LITERACY.W.9-10.7 Conduct short as well as more sustained research projects to answer a question (including a self-generated question) or solve a problem; narrow or broaden the inquiry when appropriate; synthesize multiple sources on the subject, demonstrating understanding of the subject under investigation. CCSS.ELA-LITERACY.W.9-10.8 Gather relevant information from multiple authoritative print and digital sources, using advanced searches effectively; assess the usefulness of each source in answering the research question; integrate information

(Continued)

(Continued)

Lesson Focus: Using Samples to Develop a Revision Plan and Personal Success Criteria
into the text selectively to maintain the flow of ideas, avoiding plagiarism and following a standard format for citation. CCSS.ELA-LITERACY.W.9–10.9 Draw evidence from literary or informational texts to support analysis, reflection, and research.

Purpose Statements:

- Content: Create a personal revision plan for writing.
- Language: Use a rubric, writing sample, and personal annotations on a sample essay to create a list of items to revise for your case study.
- Social: Collaborate with a peer to give feedback to others on their writing.

Success Criteria:

I can create a personal success criteria and a revision plan for my Case Study.

Text Used and Rationale:

Various excerpts from Dickenson, D., Huxtable, R., & Parker, M. (8) 2010. *The Cambridge Medical Ethics Workbook*. Cambridge: Cambridge University Press.

This text is a workbook containing multiple examples of real-life medical case studies that represent ethical dilemmas in medicine. This class is participating in a career-specific writing unit, so it is important to use models of the type of writing structure and language they are expected to produce.

Phase of Learning	Scaffolds/Supports
Show Me: Modeling/Direct Instruction **Share the purpose statements:** - Content: Create a personal revision plan for writing - Language: Use a rubric, writing sample, and personal annotations on your essay to create a list of items to work on to revise your writing - Social: Collaborate with a peer to give feedback to others on their writing **Modeling/Think Aloud:** *Welcome everyone. As you know, I received the rough drafts of your case studies a few days ago; today we are going to work on creating a personal revision plan to help you prioritize what you need to work on to refine your draft.* *To begin, I'd like you to write a list on the Post-its at your desk of the top three things you'd like to fix in your case study. Please use the rubric to help you focus on areas of need. (Figure E.2 "Case Study Rubric")* *Please take a moment to share with your partner what you are thinking you'd like to work on today. Before we start to revise and make notes on our own writing, I would like us to practice giving*	For this lesson, students will need Post-its/scratch paper, copies of the assignment rubric, and printed copies of the student sample of the Case Study. The teacher should circulate the room and give assistance to anyone struggling to name what they need to work on. Use prompts to help elicit more information or cue students to look at the rubric to help them identify areas for improvement. Sentence frames may also be provided to help students get their writing started. The sample used for this lesson should reflect the most consistent errors made by the whole class. At the end of this lesson, you will find an example of the error analysis this teacher conducted to help him compose the sample. Project or use a doc cam to show students what is happening while it is happening. Teacher should model how he annotates and gives *specific* advice on where to find help. It is also important to explicitly model that the rubric is being used to help guide the feedback. Students should write down the teacher's annotations on their own paper to serve as a model for their own as they take on more independence in the lesson.

Phase of Learning	Scaffolds/Supports
feedback to a student—Student A. With my help, you and your partner are going to give feedback to Student A on her writing. We are going to use our knowledge of our audience and the parameters of rubric to help give Student A feedback on her work without fixing all of her errors. Please take a moment to make sure you have the student sample and something to write with. *I want to show you how I look at others' writing and give them feedback that is specific and actionable. I am noticing, just glancing at the paper, that this student seems to be lacking some elements of APA format. I see that she doesn't have a header or a title, and the information at the top of the page isn't in the correct order. Since APA format is definitely graded on the rubric, I want to make sure I alert her about this.* *(Student Sample is Figure E.3 "Student Sample")* *Since I notice these errors are all very similar, I now have to decide if I am going to tell Student A to fix them one by one, or if I am going to give other related work to do.* *I want Student A to actually learn how to use APA format, so I am going to give her general feedback and a place to look for help, but I am not going to tell her exactly how to fix the issue.* *I am going to write in the margins, "Please make sure you use APA formatting; you can find a sample on our class website, or use the Little, Brown Handbook to help you find tips on formatting."* *Notice that I used the rubric and our class tools to help this student find her errors, but I didn't give her the answer. This is important because I don't want to do the work for her, but also many of you have stated that you are afraid to give specific directions in case you are wrong. Using this method will put the learning back on the writer but also not force you to give advice on a skill you might be working on yourself.*	
Help Me: Guided Practice *Now, I want you to try, with your partner, to find another error this student makes and give her feedback like I demonstrated. Please use the first body paragraph only for this. Make sure that the feedback you give is:* • *Specific* • *Actionable*	Write this list of criteria on the board so students can reference it as they work. Circulate around the class and offer prompts and cues using the following tools: • The list on the board • Rubric Assist students in small groups as needed.

(Continued)

(Continued)

Phase of Learning	Scaffolds/Supports
• *Based on the rubric* • *Followed up with a resource whenever possible* *Now that we've practiced, let's share as a class what we found. Please make sure you share what specific feedback and resources you cited as being helpful.*	Annotate along with students to help those who may have had more trouble finding the errors. If students seem ready to practice in pairs or small groups, proceed to "Collaboration." If not, practice another example or two before moving on, or form a small group for more guided instruction.
Let Us: Collaboration *With your partner, I'd now like you to give Student A feedback on the rest of her paper. Remember to use our feedback criteria, the rubric, and our classroom resources.* • *Specific* • *Actionable* • *Based on the rubric* • *Followed up with a resource whenever possible*	Students should be seated in heterogeneous pairs of two; depending on need, sentence frames may be used to help students ask questions of one another. Keep the list of feedback criteria on the board or somewhere else visible. Circulate around the class and offer prompts and cues using the following tools: • Cueing to the feedback criteria on the board when conversation lulls • Referencing the rubric if they feel they cannot find any errors • Reminding students to add comments and resources
Let Me—Independent: *Now that you've practiced giving feedback to Student A, I want you to think back to the list of revision priorities you wrote for your own paper. Student A's paper represented the top ten errors we as a class made. Using the feedback you gave as a guide, please revisit your list and reprioritize, add, or rearrange the items you need to fix to make your paper stronger.* *What you end up with will be your revision plan and new success criteria.* *As your exit ticket, please answer the following questions. Use the rubric to guide your thinking:* • *What grade would my draft earn right now?* • *After today's lesson, I would like to work on __________ .* • *Top three items I would like to work on in my writing __________ . Because __________ .* Finally, students should complete the self-assessment rubric (Figure E.5)	Give students time to look back at their lists and change any items they would like and encourage them to revisit the drafts of their own paper. Circulate and offer any assistance. You may include a model or pre-written ticket for students to see as an example:

Score	Rationale
2	Write-up: • Describes the case in question with in-depth details and textual evidence (at least two quotations) • Thoroughly introduces and explains the "ethical" dilemma • Makes a claim using reasoning regarding what should be done to best address the ethical and medical issues present in the case study • Imagines an alternative outcome using a philosopher's lens and wording/reasoning • Is two to four pages long, double spaced, Times New Roman font, and is thoroughly proofread and cited per APA format
1	Write-up: • Describes the case in question with general details and textual evidence (at least two quotations) • May superficially introduce and explain the "ethical" dilemma, but it lacks specificity • Makes a claim regarding what should be done to best address the ethical and medical issues present in the case study, but may need stronger reasoning • Is one to two pages long, double spaced, Times New Roman font, and is thoroughly proofread and cited per APA format
0	Write-up: • Fails to describe the case in question, lacks major details • Is missing the philosophical lens portion and/or has major deficiencies in this area • Is not proofread or supported properly

Mr. Ramirez   Student A

I had done a case study on Irma, a 30-year-old woman with untreatable cancer. According to the article, "she was refusing food, presented evidence of brain damage, and needed a respirator" (page 5, the Journal of Medical Ethics). This example shows that her life was not really going to be enjoyable, nor would she be able to live a regular existence. She was going to definitely be bed-ridden for her whole life and never marry or have kids. Doctors struggled with her family on the next steps they proposed to insert a feeding tube and transfer her to a complete care facility. The family wanted to take her home so she could "expire in peace." There was definitely an ethical dilemma here. According to the text it states that "Irma would most certainly end her days as a vegetable connected to vital instruments in order to survive."

In the end, the family chose to remove Irma from all fake life-producing machines. According to americanhealth.net, end of life procedures must go through a long and arduous process. "In order to stop life-saving procedures and support, the medical team in question must first submit their request to a board of ethics...the family must then provide consent in written form." If one were to look at this situation from the lens of the duty framework, they would have to consider what the "right"

(Continued)

(Continued)

thing to do is. Since that can be difficult, the hippocratic oath, "do no harm," would be the best place to start. What is more harmful in this case--keeping the patient alive with no hope for independent survival or even consciousness? Or, ending a viable life that could--against all odds--live again? In this situation, extending the life of a non-responsive person is the most harmful; it is emotionally and financially draining for the family, but also takes up resources that could be used for someone who will make a full recovery. Since a duty framework requires me to think of what I must always do and should never do, I will define my duty as honoring a life without undue suffering, so what I should never do is prolong that suffering. If the parents of the patient wanted to continue care, my duty would require me to work with them to see how their daughter is suffering unnecessarily and move towards letting her pass away naturally. Though it may be difficult, since my duty is to minimize suffering, I must do what I can within reason.

Figure E.4 • SAMPLE Error Analysis (Initials represent students who demonstrated need for competency in the skill)

Round I

Use of evidence	EG, JV, AR, TP, KG, AJ, MT
Explication of evidence	Everyone but LS, HM, DZ, BH, AR
Reasoning	Everyone but LS, HM, DZ, BH
Organization	JV, MB, AR, KG, EG, NA, KG, MA
Syntax/Language usage	HM, MA, IH, EG, JV, KG, JV, MT, KG, RS, CA, JF, TP, AR, YT, NA
APA formatting	Everyone (no one had this perfectly done)
Understanding of philosopher's approach	JV, EG, TP
Summary	JV, EG, TP, NA
Statement of Ethical Dilemma	EG, JV, TP, JF, AK, BH

Use of evidence	AR, AJ (absent on day of revision),
Explication of evidence	JV, AR, MA
Reasoning	JV, AR, MA, KG
Organization	NA, KG
Syntax/Language usage	RS, MA, NA
APA formatting	KG, AJ, KG
Understanding of philosopher's approach	EG
Summary	TP
Statement of Ethical Dilemma	None!

Figure E.5 • Self-Assessment Rubric

Teacher Name: _________________________________

Student Name: _________________________________

Category	3	2	1
Giving feedback to others	*I offered specific, actionable feedback on Student A's work. I used the rubric and our class resources to offer next steps on each element of her writing I thought needed work. I used questions in my feedback instead of giving answers.*	*I offered mostly specific feedback related to the rubric on Student A's work. I offered suggestions on where to find more help but not on every error I found. I may have also given answers instead of asking questions for a few areas.*	*I attempted to offer feedback to Student A but may have done one or more of the following:* • Failed to write comments • Did not reference the rubric • Forgot to suggest resources • Gave answers instead of help
Personal success criteria	*I completed a list of success criteria for the case study assignment that directly reflect the rubric and my specific needs and errors.*	*I completed a list of success criteria for the case study but may have elements listed that are not associated with the rubric.*	*I have listed one or two criteria but they may not be related to the rubric or they may not apply to my own writing needs or errors.*
Revision plan and self-grading	*I have self-graded my draft and have a revision plan directly connected to the rubric. I have specific steps and understanding how to fix and how I will know when I am done.*	*I have self-graded my draft and have a revision plan; there are areas that may need a stronger connection to the rubric or could use more specifics (How do I know what to fix? How will I know when I am done?).*	*I have attempted a revision plan but may be missing one of the following:* • Self-grade • Revision plan • Connection to the rubric

References

Anders, G. (2016, October 3). 14 jobs for English majors that pay at least $60,000. *Forbes.* https://www.forbes.com/sites/georgeanders/2016/10/03/14-jobs-for-english-majors-that-pay-at-least-60000/?sh=5352f6b44f1d

Applebee, A., & Langer, J. (2011). A snapshot of writing instruction in middle schools and high schools. *English Journal, 100,* 14–27.

Applebee, A. N. (1984). Writing and reasoning. *Review of Educational Research, 54*(4), 577–596.

Architectural Working Drawings. Chapter 8, p. 77. https://www.pearsonhighered.com/assets/samplechapter/0/1/3/2/0132740648.pdf

Auer, P. (2005). A postscript: Code-switching and social identity. *Journal of Pragmatics, 37*(3), 403–410.

Bailey, B. (2007). Heteroglossia and boundaries. In M. Heller (Ed.), *Bilingualism: A social approach* (pp. 257–276). Palgrave.

Bailey, S. (2015). *Academic writing: A handbook for international students.* Routledge.

Baker, A. (2014, April 27). *EMTResources.com.* Home. http://www.emtresource.com/resources/acronyms/opqrst/

Bakhtin, M. (1981). *Dialogic imagination: Four essays.* University of Texas Press.

Bean, J., Chappell, V., & Gillam, A. (2003). *Reading rhetorically.* Longman.

Brown, B. A. (2019). *Science in the city: Culturally relevant STEM education.* Harvard Education Press.

Burke, J. (2019). *The 6 academic writing assignments: Designing the user's journey.* Heinemann.

Busch, K. C. (2021). Textbooks of doubt, tested: The effect of a denialist framing on adolescents' certainty about climate change. *Environmental Education Research, 27*(11), 1574–1598. https://doi.org/10.1080/13504622.2021.1960954

Centers for Disease Control and Prevention. (2022, March 28). *Toxic substances portal.* https://www.atsdr.cdc.gov/features/toxicsubstances/index.html#atsdr-slider

Charness, N., Tuffiash, M., Krampe, R., Reingold, E., & Vasyukova, E. (2005). The role of deliberate practice in chess expertise. *Applied Cognitive Psychology, 19,* 151–165. https://doi.org/10.1002/acp.1106

Daly, J. (1978). Writing apprehension and writing competency. *Journal of Educational Research, 72*(1), 10–14.

Daly, J.A. & Miller, M.D. (1975). Apprehension of writing as a predictor of message intensity. *Journal of Psychology,* 89, 175-177.

Dover, A., & Rodriguez-Valls, F. (2022). *Radically inclusive teaching with newcomer and emergent plurilingual students: Braving up.* Teacher College Press.

Faigley, L., Daly, J., & Witte, J. (1981). The role of writing apprehension in writing performance and competence. *Journal of Educational Research, 71*(1), 17–20.

Fisher, D., & Frey, N. (2010, October). *Purpose: The foundation for high-quality teaching.* National Association of Secondary School Principals. pp. 58–61.

Fisher, D., & Frey, N. (2021). *Better learning through structured teaching.* Association for Supervision and Curriculum Development (ASCD).

Fisher, D., Frey, N., & Lapp, D. (2010). *Text complexity: Raising rigor in reading.* International Reading Association.

Gallagher, K. (2011). *Write like this: Teaching real-world writing through modeling & mentor texts.* Stenhouse Publishers.

Gallagher, K., & Anderson, J. (2012). *Writing coach: Writing and grammar for the 21st Century.* Pearson.

García, O., Lin, A. M. Y. (2017). Translanguaging in bilingual education. In O. García, A. Lin, & S. May (Eds.), *Bilingual and multilingual education.* Encyclopedia of Language and Education. Springer.

Graham, S. (2019). Changing how writing is taught. *Review of Research in Education, 43*(1), 277–303. https://doi.org/10.3102/0091732X18821125

Graham, S., & Perin, D. (2007). *Writing next: Effective strategies to improve writing of adolescents in middle and high school. A report to the*

Carnegie Corporation of New York. Alliance for Excellence in Education. https://www.carnegie .org/media/filer_public/3c/f5/3cf58727-34f4 -4140-a014-723a00ac56f7/ccny_report_2007 _writing.pdf

Grant, M., Lapp, D., Fisher, D., Johnson, K., & Frey, N. (2012). Purposeful instruction: Mixing up the "I", "We", and "You". *Journal of Adolescent and Adult Literacy, 56*(1), 45–55. http://onlineli brary.wiley.com/doi/10.1002/JAAL.00101/ abstract

Gumperz, J. J. (1982). *Discourse strategies.* Cambridge University.

Hart, B., & Risley, T. (2003). The early catastrophe. *Education Review, 17*(1), 110–118.

Hattie, J. (2008). *Visible learning: A synthesis of over 800 meta-analyses relating to achievement.* Routledge.

Hattie, J. (2020). *Visualizing learning for teachers: Maximizing impact on learning.* Routledge.

Hattie, J. (2022). *Barometer of influence.* https://visible-learning.org/2022/01/ hatties-barometer-of-influence-infographic/

Hattie, J. (2023). *Visible Learning: The sequel. A synthesis of over 2100 meta-analyses relating to achievement.* New York, NY: Routledge.

Hayes, J. R., & Flower, L. S. (1986). Writing research and the writer. *American Psychologist, 41*(10), 1106–1113.

Human Factor. (n.d.). *Lightcast.* Retrieved March 2, 2023, from https://lightcast.io/ human-factor-soft-skills

Joos, M. (1962). *Five clocks.* Harcourt.

Land, C. A. (2022). Recentering purpose and audience as part of a critical, Humanizing approach to writing instruction. *Reading Research Quarterly, 57*(1), 37–58. https://doi .org/10.1002/rrq.371

Lapp, D., Thayre, M., Wolsey, T.D., Fisher, D. (2014). Arguments are only as credible as their sources: Teaching students to choose wisely. E-ssentials. https://www.literacyworldwide.org/ get-resources/ila-e-ssentials/8056

Light, R. (2001). *Making the most of college.* Harvard University Press.

Marzano, R. J. (2009). *Becoming a reflective teacher.* Solution Tree Press.

McCarthy, P., Meier, S., & Rinderer, R. (1985). Self-Efficacy and writing: A different view of self-evaluation. *College Composition and Communication, 36*(4), 465–471.

Morrison, T. (2017). *Language registers and language varieties.* Jamaica Gleaner.

Myers-Scotton, C. (2005*). Multiple voices: An introduction to bilingualism.* Blackwell Publishing.

National Reading Panel (US). (2000). *Report of the National Reading Panel: Teaching children to read: An evidence-based assessment of the scientific research literature on reading and its implications for reading instruction: Reports of the subgroups.* National Institute of Child Health and Human Development, National Institutes of Health.

NCTE. (2022, April 25). *Media Education in English language arts.* Retrieved June 14, 2022, from https://ncte.org/statement/media_education/

Nonko, E. (2016). *A guide to architect terms and phrases.* https://www.curbed.com/2016/7/11/12149096/ architecture-glossary-architect-terms

North Carolina State University. (2021, September 13). *Uncertainty on climate change in textbooks linked to uncertainty in students.* ScienceDaily. Retrieved April 1, 2022, from www.sciencedaily .com/releases/2021/09/210913135644.htm

Place, A. (2022). *Spell check please! The 10 most commonly misspelled words on resumes.* https:// www.benefitnews.com/list/most-commonly -misspelled-words-on-resumes

Rodriguez-Valls, F. Personal communication, February 15, 2023.

Sanchez, C. E., Atkinson, K. M., Koenka, A. C., Moshontz, H., & Cooper, H. (2017). Self-grading and peer-grading for formative and summative assessments in 3rd through 12th grade classrooms: A meta-analysis. *Journal of Educational Psychology, 109*(8), 1049–1066.

Schmoker, M. (2022, June 3). No, fewer books, less writing won't add up to Media Literacy (opinion). *Education Week.* Retrieved June 14, 2022, from https://www.edweek.org/teaching-learn ing/opinion-no-fewer-books-less-writing- wont-add-up-to-media-literacy/2022/06

Shanahan, T., & Shanahan, C. (2008). Teaching disciplinary literacy to adolescents: Rethinking Content Area Literacy. *Harvard Educational Review, 78*(1), 40–59.

Swales, J. M. (1988). Discourse communities, genres and English as an international language. *World Englishes, 7,* 211–220.

Torrent Tucker, D. (2020, November 19). *Stanford researchers explore potential for kelp to relieve ocean acidification.* Stanford News Service. Retrieved December 6, 2022, from

https://news.stanford.edu/press-releases/2020/11/19/kelp-help-relievan-acidification/

vanGog, T., Ericsson, K. A., Rikers, R. M. J. P., & Paas, F. (2005). Instructional design for advanced learners: Establishing connections between the theoretical frameworks of cognitive load and deliberate practice. *Educational Technology Research and Development, 53*(3), 73–81.

Wiggins, G., & McTighe, J. (2005). *Understanding by design* (2nd ed.). Association for Supervision and Curriculum Development (ASCD).

Wilson-Lopez, A., & Bean, T. (2017). Content area and disciplinary literacy. *Literacy Leadership Brief.* https://www.literacyworldwide.org/docs/default-source/where-we-stand/ila-content-area-disciplinary-literacy-strategies-frameworks.pdf?sfvrsn=e180a58e_6

Wilste, E. (2006). Using Writing to Predict Students' Choice of Majors. *Journalism & Mass Communication Educator, 61*(2), 179–194.

Wolsey, T. D., & Lapp, D. (2017). *Literacy in the disciplines: A teacher's guide for grades 5–12.* Guilford Press.

Wolsey, T. D., Lapp, D., Grant, M., & Karkouti, I. (2019). Intersections of literacy and teaching with the disciplines and professions: We asked some experts. *Journal of Adolescent and Adult Literacy, 63*(3), 251-256.

Index

Helping educators make the greatest impact

CORWIN HAS ONE MISSION: to enhance education through intentional professional learning.

We build long-term relationships with our authors, educators, clients, and associations who partner with us to develop and continuously improve the best evidence-based practices that establish and support lifelong learning.

Because...
ALL TEACHERS ARE LEADERS

AFRIKA AFENI MILLS

This guide explores why racial identity work is crucial, especially for White-identifying students and teachers, and guides educators to provide opportunities for antiracist learning.

ALLISON SKERRETT, PETER SMAGORINSKY

Engage students in critical thinking literacy activities, and inquiry using the personal and social issues of pressing importance to today's students.

MARIA WALTHER

This resource offers a scaffolding for moving from teacher-led demonstration of read alouds to student-led discovery of literacy skills—across the bridge of shared reading.

VERA AHIYYA

Spark courageous conversations with children about race, identity, and social justice using read alouds as an entry point.

To order your copies, visit corwin.com/literacy

At Corwin Literacy we have put together a collection of just-in-time, classroom-tested, practical resources from trusted experts that allow you to quickly find the information you need when you need it.

DOUGLAS FISHER, NANCY FREY, DIANE LAPP

Like an animated encyclopedia, this book delivers the latest evidence-based practices in 13 interactive modules that will transform your instruction and reenergize your career.

JUSTIN M. STYGLES

Learn how to build relationships so shame-bound readers trust enough to risk enough to grow.

GRETCHEN BERNABEI, JAYNE HOVER

Use these lessons and concrete text structures designed to help students write self-generated commentary in response to reading.

CHRISTINA NOSEK, MELANIE MEEHAN, MATTHEW JOHNSON, MATTHEW R. KAY, DAVE STUART JR.

This series offers actionable answers to your most pressing questions about teaching reading, writing, and ELA.